HISTORY OF INDIA

HISTORY OF INDIA

Edited by
A. V. WILLIAMS JACKSON, Ph. D., LL.D.

VOLUME IV

From the Reign of Akbar the Great to the Fall of the Moghul Empire

BY
Stanley Lane-Poole, M.A. Litt.D.
M.R.I.A.

GYAN

Published by

GYAN

Gyan Publishing House
5, Ansari Road
Daryaganj, New Delhi-110002
Phone: 011-47034999, 9811692060
E-mail: books@gyanbooks.com

Distribution Network
gyanbooks.com
India, USA, Canada, UK, Australia, France

ISBN : 978-81-212-6772-4 (Set)
978-81-212-6769-4 (PB)
First Published, 1906

2nd Impression 2022

Printed at: Gyan Press, Delhi.

HISTORY OF INDIA (VOL. IV)

Author: Stanley Lane - Poole

The Taj Mahal at Agra

The Taj Mahal at Agra is acknowledged to be one of the wonders of the world, and is thought by many to be the most beautiful building ever erected by man. Even the most lavish praises that have been bestowed upon it fail still to do justice to the exquisite charm of its construction and surroundings, which can be fully appreciated only by seeing it; and all who have visited it are ready to concede that no more perfect monument in marble has been erected to the memory of a woman than this beautiful edifice dedicated by the Moghul emperor, Shah Jahan, to Mumtaz-i-Mahal, his beloved wife.

History of India

Edited by

A. V. WILLIAMS JACKSON, Ph. D., LL. D.
Professor of Indo-Iranian Languages in Columbia University

VOLUME IV

Mediæval India from the Mohammedan Conquest to the Reign of Akbar the Great

By

STANLEY LANE-POOLE, M. A., Litt. D., M. R. I. A.
Professor of Arabic at Trinity College, Dublin

INTRODUCTION BY THE EDITOR

WHEN Akbar the Great, the contemporary of Queen Elizabeth, ascended the throne of India, it was with a heart inspired by the highest ideals ever held by a ruler of Islamitic blood, and the manner in which he lived up to these ideals made him the noblest monarch, after Asoka, that ever reigned over the land beyond the river Indus.

Akbar was followed by his son Jahangir, the Great Moghul, and he by Shah Jahan, the Magnificent, who was succeeded in turn by Aurangzib, the Puritan Emperor and last of the line of great Moghuls. Mohammedan India reached the culmination of its glory in the fortunes of this dynasty. The subsequent rise of the Marathas heralded a new era, and signs of the beginnings of European power in India were now at hand.

The interesting story of these events, as told by Professor Lane-Poole, has been supplemented by including in this volume two selections from native Mohammedan chroniclers found in that inexhaustible mine of material, Elliot's "History of India as Told by Its Own

Historians" in Professor Dowson's edition, the indebtedness to which is acknowledged.

With reference to the preparation of the text of the present volume editorially and with regard to the illustrations, I have been guided in general by the principles laid down in the preceding volumes of the series. Besides the assistance previously acknowledged in respect to illustrative material and other matter, I desire to unite with the publishers in thanking Mr. Frederick J. Agate, of New York, who was with me in my travels through India, for the use of certain photographs in his collection, and also to thank Dr. Edward S. Holden, Librarian of the United States Military Academy at West Point, for the pictures of two Mohammedan heroines, Nur Jahan and Mumtaz-i-Mahal, reproduced from miniatures in the British Museum, through the courtesy of Messrs. Charles Scribner's Sons, of New York.

A. V. WILLIAMS JACKSON.

CONTENTS

LIST OF ILLUSTRATIONS

CUIRASS, MADE OF HIDE COVERED WITH VELVET, AND STUDDED WITH NAILS.

CHAPTER I

THE UNITED EMPIRE

AKBAR THE GREAT

1556-1605 A. D.

THE long reign of Akbar, which lasted from 1556 to 1605, has been represented as the golden age of the Moghul empire. It was in reality but the beginning of the period of splendour which ended with the disastrous wars of Aurangzib. Akbar was the true founder and organizer of the empire, but it is too often forgotten that it took him twenty years of hard fighting to bring Hindustan under subjection, and that even at his death the process was incomplete. There was no sudden and miraculous submission to the boy of thirteen who found himself called to an as yet unconquered throne by the accident that ended his father's ineffectual life in the beginning of 1556. A hard struggle was before him ere he could call himself king even of Delhi. He was fortunate, no doubt, in the divisions of his adversaries, and after the crushing defeat of Himu at Panipat he was never called upon to meet a general muster of Indian troops; but the process of reducing usurper after usurper, and suppressing one rebellion after another, was tedious and harassing, and in spite of a wise statesmanship matured by experience, and a clemency and toleration which grew with advancing years, to the day of his death Akbar seldom knew what it was to enjoy a year's freedom from war.

At the time of his accession the only parts of India that he possessed were the Panjab and Delhi in the north, which were the fruits of the victory at Sirhind in 1555. The Afghan dynasty still held Bengal and the Ganges valley; the Rajputs were independent in Western Hindustan, and there were innumerable chiefs in possession of separate principalities all over the country. It was not till the third year of his reign that Akbar was able to occupy Ajmir. Gwalior fell in 1558, and by 1561 he had driven the Afghans back from Lucknow and Jaunpur. The Moghul empire so far was almost restricted to the Panjab and the Northwest Provinces, though Malwa was partly overrun in 1561, and Burhanpur in Khandesh was captured a year later.

The storming of Chitor in 1567 was a conspicuous landmark in history, but it was not till 1572 that the Rajputs were finally brought into the empire. Bengal was not conquered before 1575, and Gujarat, though occupied in 1572, had to be retaken in 1584 and gave trouble for several years more. Kabul, under Akbar's brother Hakim, was almost a separate kingdom and frequently aggressive. Among the outlying provinces, Orissa became part of the empire as late as 1590, Kashmir in 1587, Sind in 1592, Kandahar in 1594, and only a small portion of the Deccan was annexed in Akbar's life.

The reign was thus a perpetual series of efforts toward the expansion of a territory originally small. So doubtful indeed seemed Akbar's prospects of Indian sovereignty at the moment when his father's unexpected death placed him in command, that in the first council of war the generals strongly urged an immediate retreat upon Kabul, and their advice was overruled only by the firm decision of the regent Bairam, an old Turkman officer who had followed Babar and Humayun, and realized better than the others the divided and leaderless state of the enemy. Matters were certainly in an alarming position. Sikandar of Delhi had been driven to the mountains, where he held Mankot against all attacks, but a far more formidable army was marching to take vengeance. Himu, the general of the Bengal kingdom, a Hindu who had rapidly advanced from a mere shopkeeper to practically supreme power, entered Agra unopposed, defeated Tardi Beg at Delhi, occupied the capital, assumed the historic title of Raja Vikramajit, and then advanced to crush the Moghul forces.

When the dispirited remnant of the garrison of Delhi reached Akbar's headquarters at Sirhind, news had just arrived of another blow, the revolt of Kabul. Fortunately the young emperor had a great soldier at his side to meet the crisis. Bairam, the atalik, or regent, was a consummate general and a man of iron resolution. He instantly made an example of Tardi Beg, for the loss of Delhi, and placed the other disgraced officers under arrest. Then he sent on the advance-guard, which was lucky enough to intercept the entire park of Ottoman artillery which Himu had incautiously set adrift; and on Friday the 5th of November, 1556, the two armies confronted each other on the field of Panipat, where thirty years before Babar had overthrown the Afghan power, and where two centuries later another battle swept away the Maratha hordes and prepared the way for England.

In spite of the loss of his guns, Himu commanded a force sufficient to dismay the Moghul leaders. He had three divisions, the centre of which was composed of twenty thousand horse (Afghans and Rajputs) supported by five hundred elephants, and the whole force of elephantry numbered at least 1500. Himu led the advance, "scowling on his elephant Hawa, 'the Wind.'" His charge upon the Moghul left was successful; he then turned to crush their centre. But here the archers stood firm, the enemy were harassed by showers of arrows, and one fortunate shaft pierced the eye of the Hindu leader. There was no one in authority to take up the command, and the masterless crowd broke up like a herd of stampeded horses. Himu on his elephant was driven straight into the presence of Akbar, and Bairam bade the boy flesh his sword on the dying "infidel." The honourable chivalry which distinguished Akbar above all his line at once burst forth: "How can I strike a man who is as good as dead?" he cried. Bairam had no such fine scruples, and immediately dispatched the wounded man.

The crisis had been bravely met, and Akbar had never again to confront so dangerous an enemy. Henceforward, though constantly fighting, he had the advantage—incalculable in Oriental warfare—of being in the position of the attacker, not the attacked. Delhi again opened its gates and received him with effusive loyalty. Agra followed the example of the capital, and after an eight months' siege Sikandar surrendered Mankot and retired to Bengal. The young prince was now king at least in the northwest corner of India. The process of settling this comparatively small territory and dealing with the revenues and the status of the military vassals occupied the next few years, and, except for the reduction of the great fortress of Gwalior and the conquest of the Ganges valley as far as Jaunpur and Benares, the limits of the kingdom were not greatly extended.

In 1560 Akbar took the reins into his own hands. He had chafed under the masterful management of Bairam, whose severity and jealousy had been shown in several high-handed executions and had roused general discontent. Palace intrigue set Akbar's mind against his old tutor, who was doubtless slow to realize that his pupil was no longer a child to be held by a

THE PALACE AT GWALIOR.

leading-string. In an Eastern harem there are powerful influences against which few ministers can prevail, and Akbar's foster-mother, Maham Anaga, ruled the palace in those early years. She used her power to undermine the emperor's esteem for Bairam. Taking advantage of a visit to Delhi, where he was free from the regent's domination, she worked upon his natural impatience of the regent's arrogance, and induced him to break his bonds. Akbar publicly announced that he had taken the government into his own hands, and sent orders to the deposed minister to go on pilgrimage to Mekka—a courteous form of temporary banishment. The young emperor might, perhaps, have dealt more gently with the honoured servant of his father and grandfather—one, too, who had so strenuously served him in his hour of peril—but the change had to be made, and it could not be easy in any way. Bairam left for Gujarat to take a boat for Arabia, but on his way he fell among evil counsellors who tempted him to revolt. He was defeated and made humble submission, when Akbar instantly pardoned him with all his old kindness. But there could now be no place for Bairam in the government, and he set forth sadly on his pilgrimage, once the chief desire of the staunch Moslem, but now a mark of his downfall. Before he could embark he was assassinated by an Afghan in quittance of a blood-feud.

The nurse's triumph was brief. For a time she acted almost as a prime minister, and her quick intelligence, as well as her devotion to her foster-son, made her invaluable to him. Unhappily, her hopes were wrapped up in her own son, Adham Khan. She pushed him forward to high command, which he filled with more arrogance than loyalty; he fell into disgrace, and when finally out of envy and chagrin he murdered

Akbar's foster-father, the prime minister Shams-ad-din, in 1563, and then stood at the door of the harem as if in sanctuary, his cup was full. The emperor rushed out, sword in hand, felled the assassin with a blow of his fist, and, foster-brother though he was, Adham was instantly thrown over the battlements of the palace. It broke his mother's heart, and she survived him but forty days.

It was time that Akbar freed himself from this harem influence. Adham had already tarnished the emperor's name in Malwa, where, after expelling the pleasure-loving and cultured Afghan governor, Baz Bahadur, he behaved grossly toward the vanquished. "Baz Bahadur," writes Elphinstone, "had a Hindu mistress who is said to have been one of the most beautiful women ever seen in India. She was as accomplished as she was fair, and was celebrated for her verses in the Hindi language. She fell into the hands of Adham Khan on the flight of Baz Bahadur, and, finding herself unable to resist his importunities and threatened violence, she appointed an hour to receive him, put on her most splendid dress, on which she sprinkled the richest perfumes, and lay down on a couch with her mantle drawn over her face. Her attendants thought that she had fallen asleep, but on endeavouring to awake her on the approach of the khan, they found she had taken poison and was already dead." Nor was this all. Other ladies of Baz Bahadur's harem were in Adham's possession, and when Akbar himself rode to Malwa in hot haste and bitter shame to stop his lieutenant's atrocities, Maham Anaga had these innocent women killed, lest they should tell tales to the emperor. Akbar was well quit of both mother and son.

Although the young emperor was still immature, and it was many years before he entered upon that stage of philosophic enlightenment which has made his name a household word for wisdom and toleration, he had already shown something of his character and self-reliance. His refusal to strike the dying Himu,

GOLD COINS OF AKBAR AT AGRA, A. H. 981, (A. D. 1573).

his firm and yet not unkind treatment of his revolted regent, his honest indignation at Adham's iniquities, show that Akbar possessed the right spirit. Physically he is described by his son Jahangir, in later life, as of middle stature, long in the arms and sturdy of figure, rather sallow in face, with black eyes and eyebrows and an open forehead. A wart on the left side of his nose was regarded as not only auspicious but exceedingly beautiful. His voice was ringing, and, in spite of scant culture, his conversation had a charm of its own. " His manners and habits," adds his son, " were quite different from those of other people, and his countenance was full of godlike dignity." His mode of life was regular and abstemious. His time was carefully filled, and he slept little; "his sleep looked more like waking." He ate but one meal a day, and that in moderation, never approaching satiety. Ganges water, "cooled with saltpetre," was his drink, and it was kept sealed for fear of poison. He took meat but twice a week, and even then with repugnance, for he disliked making his body a "tomb for beasts"; but some meat he found necessary to support his fatigues. He was a man of great energy and constant occupation, capable of immense and prolonged effort, and fond of all manly exercises. He was a fine polo player and so devoted to the game that he used to play it even by night, using fireballs. The chase was his keenest delight, and he would break the tedium of the long marches of his many campaigns by hunting elephants or tigers on the way. We read of 350 elephants taken in a single day; at another time he stalked wild asses for thirty-five miles, and shot sixteen. He had names for his guns, and kept records of their performances. There were vast battues, when thousands of deer, nil-gau, or Indian blue antelope, jackals, and foxes were driven by the beaters in a circle of forty miles, and the lines drawn closer and closer, till Akbar could enjoy at his ease several days' shooting and hawking with plenty of sport, and still leave a few thousand head for his followers to practise on. These battues sometimes took place by night, and there is a curious painting of the period, showing one of these nocturnal hunts with the emperor on horseback, and the game, startled by the bright flashing of a lantern, leaping as the chief shikar, or huntsman, draws his bow. Akbar had also mechanical genius. He devised a new method of making gun-barrels of spirally rolled iron, which could not burst; he invented a machine which cleaned sixteen barrels at once, another by which seventeen guns could be fired simultaneously with one match, and there were many more things that he improved by his talent for invention.

THE DAULAT BAGH, AJMIR.

Nothing seemed to fatigue Akbar. He is said to have ridden from Ajmir to Agra, a distance of 240 miles, in a day and a night, and even if (with some authorities) we double the time, it is still wonderful travelling, and one is not surprised to read that he often exhausted his horses when pushing on night and day at breakneck speed. He liked to see a good fight, too, and one day at Thanesar he chanced upon a curious spectacle. It was the annual festival, and there was a vast crowd beside the sacred lake; the holy men were gathering a rich harvest in charity, when the customary struggle arose between two sects of fanatics for the possession of the bathing-place. They came to the emperor and begged to be allowed to fight it out according to their habit. He consented, and allowed some of his soldiers to smear their bodies with ashes and go in to support the weaker side. There was a splendid fight; many were killed, we are told; and "the emperor greatly enjoyed the sight."

On a campaign Akbar was indefatigable. In one of his pursuits of Ali Kuli Khan-zaman, an Uzbeg officer who repeatedly revolted in the name of Akbar's jealous brother, Hakim, and was as often pardoned by his too forgiving sovereign, he pushed on so rapidly that of his army only five hundred men and elephants succeeded in being in at the finish. In spite of his reduced force, Akbar rode straight for the enemy, and took his own share of the fighting. "As the battle grew hot, the emperor alighted from his elephant, Bal-sundar, and mounted a horse. Then he gave orders for the elephants to be driven against the lines of Ali Kuli Khan. Among them there was an elephant named Hiranand, and when he approached the ranks of the enemy, they let loose against him an elephant called Diyana; but Hiranand gave him such a butt that he fell upon the spot. Ali Kuli received a wound from an arrow, and while he was drawing it out another struck his horse. The animal became restive, and Ali Kuli was thrown. An elephant named Narsing now came up and was about to crush him, when Ali Kuli cried out to the driver, 'I am a great man; if you take me alive to the emperor he will reward you.' The driver paid no heed to his words, but drove the animal over him and crushed him under foot." Many prisoners were cast to the elephants to be trampled to death, a common mode of execution in India, in which Akbar showed no scruple. After refusing, in his chivalrous way, to attack an unprepared enemy till the trumpets had announced his approach, he had no qualms about making a pyramid of two thousand rebels' heads after the fashion of his ancestor Timur. He could be terribly stern and was subject to paroxysms of rage, in one of which he threw a servant from the battlements for falling asleep in the palace, but his natural inclination was ever towards mercy, and his forgiveness often cost him dear.

As an example of personal courage his attack on his rebellious cousins, the Mirzas, at Surat in 1572 may be instanced. Pressing on at his usual speed, he found himself on the bank of the Mahindri River in face of the enemy, with only forty men at his back. Sixty more soon joined him, and with this handful he forthwith swam the river, stormed the town, and, rushing through, discovered the enemy in a plain on the other side. The emperor's force was outmatched by ten to one, and the fighting was desperate. "The royal forces were in a narrow place, hedged in with thorns, where three horsemen could not pass abreast. The emperor with much courage was at the front, with Raja Bhagvan Das beside him. Three of the enemy's horsemen now charged them. One attacked the raja, who hurled his spear at him and wounded him as he was entangled in the thorns, so that he fled; the other two attacked his Majesty, who received them so stoutly that they were forced to make off." Two officers now joined Akbar, who, refusing their escort, sent them after his assailants; and the little force, roused by their emperor's danger, utterly routed the enemy. The courage of Akbar had put every man on his mettle, and the victors returned to Baroda the heroes of the hour. In the campaign of 1572-3 Akbar not only retook Ahmadabad and entered Cambay and Baroda, but captured the strong fort of Surat, which had been built with extraordinary care and skill to keep out the Portuguese, and contained mortars bearing the name of Sulaiman the Great of Turkey. When Akbar took the fort of Junagarh in Kathiawar in 1591, he found there a gun of the same Sultan, whose fleet had vainly attacked the coast castles and had been forced to abandon the guns.

The presence of the Raja Bhagvan Das at Akbar's side in the skirmish just described is significant. If he had not been altogether successful in managing his Mohammedan followers, a turbulent body of adventurers, the emperor more than redeemed his overindulgence to rebellious Moslems by his wise conciliation of Hindus. It may be that the very truculence and insubordination which he found so hard to check among his Turkish officers threw him perforce into the arms of the Rajputs; for we can hardly believe that a mere lad, brought up in an atmosphere of despotic rule, could as yet have imagined the ideal of a government resting upon the loyalty of the native population. As early as 1562 Bhagvan's father, Raja Bihari Mal, the lord of Amber and ancestor of the present maharajas of Jaipur, had come to pay his homage to the new sovereign. "He was received with great honour and consideration, and his daughter, an honourable lady, was accepted by his Majesty, and took her place among the ladies of the court." Akbar had already married his cousins Rukayya and Salima, but this union with a Rajput princess marked a new policy. Her father was decorated with the highest rank of the official aristocracy, as a mansabdar, or general of five thousand horse, and the bride, freely exercising the rites of her own faith and performing the usual Hindu sacrifices, encouraged her husband's tendency towards religious toleration. Later on he took other women, Hindu, Persian, Moghul, and even an Armenian, until his harem formed a parliament of religions, though no rumour of their probable debates ever reached the outside world. Abu-l-Fazl says there were more than five thousand inmates of the harem, in various capacities, and sagely remarks that "the large number of women—a vexatious question even for great statesmen—furnished his Majesty with an opportunity to display his wisdom."

An almost immediate result of this alliance with the Rajput princess was the abolition in 1562 of the *jizya*, or poll-tax, which Mohammedan conquerors levied upon unbelievers in accordance with the law of Islam. His next act was to discontinue the tax upon

Hindu pilgrims, on the ground that, however superstitious the rites of pilgrimage might be, it was wrong to place any obstacle in the way of man's service to God. No more popular measures could have been enacted. The jizya was an insult as well as a burden, and both taxes bore heavily on the poor and were bitterly

AGRA GATE, FATHPUR-SIKRI.

resented. It was the reimposition of the tax on religion in the time of Aurangzib that, more than anything else, uprooted the wise system established by his ancestor. But while conciliating the Hindus by just and equal government, Akbar did not hesitate to interfere with some of their most cherished practices when they offended his sense of humanity. He forbade child-marriage, trial by ordeal, and animal sacrifice; he permitted widows to marry again, and set his face resolutely against the burning of widows on their husband's pyres: wholly to abolish *suttee* was beyond his power, but he ordained that the sacrifice must be voluntary, and he took personal pains to see that no compulsion should be used. He also insisted that "the consent of the bride and bridegroom and the permission of the parents are absolutely necessary in marriage contracts"—a new idea in a country where girls were married without regard for their own wishes or desires.

Akbar was too shrewd a man to suppose that the hereditary pride of the Rajputs was to be conquered merely by kind words and mild measures. He knew that often the best way to make friends with a man is to knock him down. Udai Singh, the great rana of Mewar (son of Sanga, Babar's adversary), left him in no doubt as to his hostility. He sheltered Baz Bahadur when driven from Malwa by the imperial army, and when other rajas came and tendered their allegiance to the Moghul, Udai Singh stood aloof, apparently secure in his rocky fortresses and numerous array of troops and elephants. Akbar, he thought, could never take his strong castle of Chitor, standing on an isolated crag, four hundred feet high, and with almost perpendicular sides towards the top. The summit was occupied by an immense fortress, well supplied with provisions, wells, and water-tanks, and garrisoned by eight thousand veterans of the Rajput race under a famous leader, Jai Mal, the rana himself having prudently retreated to the Aravali hills on Akbar's approach in 1567.

The citadel in Akbar's time is thus described by Mulla Ahmad: "The castle is situated in the midst of a level plain which has no other hills. The mountain is twelve miles round at the base, and nearly six at the summit. On the east and north it is faced with hard stone, and the garrison had no fears on those sides, nor could guns, swivels, stone-slings, or mangonels do much damage on the other sides, if they managed to reach them. Travellers do not mention any fortress like this in all the world. The whole summit was crowded with buildings, some several stories high, and the battlements were strongly guarded and the magazines full." The garrison laughed at the slender force of three or four thousand which the emperor had brought against a fortress twelve miles in girth, and well they might.

They had to deal with a skilful engineer, however, and Akbar made his dispositions with great care. Batteries were set up all around the fort, and a strict blockade was established. Meanwhile generals were sent to seize Rampur and Udaipur, and to lay the surrounding country waste. "From day to day," says Mulla Ahmad, "the gallant assailants brought their attacks closer to the fort on every side, though many fell under the resolute fire of the defenders. Orders were given for digging trenches and making *sabats*, and nearly five thousand builders, carpenters, masons, smiths, and sappers were mustered from all parts.

LAKE AT UDAIPUR.

Sabats, or broad covered ways, under the shelter of which the besiegers approach a fortress protected from gun and musket fire, are contrivances peculiar to Hindustan, for the strong forts of that land are full of guns, muskets, and defensive machines, and can be taken only by this means. Two sabats were accordingly begun; one, opposite the royal quarters, was so broad and high that two elephants and two horses could easily pass abreast, with raised spears. The sabats were begun from the brow of the hill (*i. e.* half-way up, below the perpendicular scarp), which is a fortress upon a fortress." Seven or eight thousand horsemen and gunners strove to stop the work, and in spite of the bull-hide roofs over the labourers, a hundred or so were killed every day, and their corpses were used as building materials. There was no forced labour, by Akbar's order, but the volunteers were stimulated by showers of money. Soon one of the sabats overtopped the wall of the castle, and on the roof of it a gallery was made whence the emperor could watch the fight.

Meanwhile the sappers had not been idle. Two bastions were mined with gunpowder, and a storming party was drawn up. The first mine blew a bastion into the air, and the stormers rushed into the breach, shouting their war-cry, and were at once at hand-grip with the garrison. At that moment the second mine, owing to a miscalculation, exploded and hurled in fragments into the air the crowd struggling in the breach. The charge was so heavy that stones and corpses were hurled " miles " away, according to the historian, and the royal army was half blinded by the dust and smoke and by the hail of stones and bodies that descended upon them.

The first approach had failed, and Akbar now ordered the other sabat to be pushed forward. He was more resolved than ever to take the fort by storm "so that in future no other fortress should dare to withstand him." He took up his position in the gallery on the top of the sabat, as before, armed with his musket, "deadly as the darts of fate, with which he killed every moving thing that caught his eye." At last the walls were breached, and the assault was ordered. Jai Mal, the commandant, "an infidel, yet valiant," struggled bravely in every part and all day long, encouraging his men to beat off the enemy. At the hour of evening prayer he came in front of the royal battery, where Akbar sat discharging his gun "Sangram" as often as light flashed forth in the bastion. Jai Mal happened to be standing in the tower encouraging his men just when a blaze of light revealed his face to Akbar, who fired and killed him on the spot. Then the garrison gave up hope, and after burning the body of their leader, they performed their dismal rite of *jauhar*, burning all their families and goods in huge bonfires, and then rushing on to death. The besiegers saw the flare of the pyres, and poured through the breaches, while Akbar looked on from the top of the sabat. Three elephants he sent into the castle to aid in the general massacre of the devoted garrison. The Rajputs fought every step; each lane and street and bazar was sternly disputed; they fought up to the very temple. Two thousand were killed by midday; the total death-roll of the Hindus was at least eight thousand men, besides their families; the rest were made prisoners, as we know from the accounts of those who were present at the storming. The heroism of the defence was long commemorated in popular tradition by the two statues, supposed to represent Jai Mal and his brother, mounted on stone elephants, which flanked the gate of the fortress at Delhi. "These two elephants," says Bernier, "mounted by the two heroes, have an air of grandeur and inspire me with an awe and respect which I cannot describe."

The fall of Chitor, followed by two other famous fortresses, Rantambhor and Kalinjar, a few months later, secured the allegiance of the Rajputs. The rajas agreed to acclaim a power which they found as irresistible as it was just and tolerant. Akbar cemented the good feeling by marrying another princess, daughter of the raja of Bikanir, and henceforward he could rely on the loyalty of the most splendid soldiery in India. In his future campaigns, as in those of his son and grandson, there were always brave Hindus to the fore, and the names of Bhagvan Das, Man Singh, and Todar Mal are famous in the annals of Moghul warfare and administration. Bhagvan Das and Man Singh not only distinguished themselves in the wearisome and reiterated campaigns which the unsettled state of Gujarat compelled Akbar to undertake for a space of twenty years, but were even trusted by him in 1578 to wage war upon the ever hostile rana of Udaipur, Rajput against Rajput. They justified his confidence, drove the rana to the Indus, and captured his strongholds of Goganda and Kunbhalmir.

CHAPTER II

AKBAR'S REFORMS

THE DIVINE FAITH

1566-1605 A.D.

THIS assimilation of the Hindu chiefs was the most conspicuous feature of Akbar's reign. His wars were like other Indian wars, only mitigated by his sovereign quality of mercy to those who submitted, and by his scrupulous care that the peasants should not suffer by the passage of his troops. The empire was gradually extended till it stretched from Kandahar to the Bay of Bengal, and included the whole of Hindustan down to the Narbada. But the remarkable points about this expansion to the old limits of Ala-addin's realm were, first, that it was done with the willing help of the Hindu princes, and, secondly, that expansion went hand in hand with orderly administration. This was a new thing in Indian government, for hitherto the local officials had done pretty much as it pleased them, and the central authority had seldom interfered so long as the revenue did not suffer. Akbar allowed no oppression by his lieutenants, and not a few of his campaigns were undertaken mainly for the purpose of punishing governors who had been guilty of self-seeking and peculation. Much of the improvement was due to his employment of Hindus, who at that time were better men of business than the uneducated and mercenary adventurers who formed a large proportion of the Mohammedan invaders.

No Moslem served Akbar more zealously or with more far-reaching results than the great financier, Raja Todar Mal, a Khatri Rajput, who had served in his youth under the able administration of Sher Shah, and had thus gained priceless experience in the management of lands and revenues. He assisted Akbar's first chancellor of the exchequer, Muzaffar Khan, in settling the newly acquired kingdom, and in 1566 took a leading part in suppressing the revolt of Ali Kuli. It was the first time, in Moghul rule, that a Hindu had been sent against a Moslem enemy, and his employment was doubtless due to Akbar's suspicion that the Mohammedan generals might act in collusion with their old comrade, the rebel. After this he was employed in settling the revenue system of Gujarat, and then again took military command in the conquest of Bengal in 1574-7 and its reduction in 1581, when he distinguished himself by his firm courage. He was rewarded soon afterwards with the office of vizir, and in 1582 became chief finance minister, introducing the famous reforms and the new assessment known as Todar Mal's rent-roll, the Domesday Book of the Moghul empire. He died in 1589. "Careful to keep himself from selfish ambition," writes Abu-l-Fazl, "he devoted himself to the service of the state, and earned an everlasting fame."

There is no name in mediæval history more renowned in India to the present day than that of Todar Mal, and the reason is that nothing in Akbar's reforms more nearly touched the welfare of the people than the great financier's reconstruction of the revenue system. The land-tax was always the main source of revenue in India, and it had become almost the sole universal burden since Akbar had abolished not only the poll-tax and pilgrims' dues but over fifty minor duties. The object was now to levy a fair rent on the land, which should support the administration without unduly burdening the cultivators. Mr. H. G. Keene, an able modern Indian administrator, thus describes the system: "The basis of the land-revenue was the recognition that the agriculturist was the owner of the soil, the state being entitled to the surplus produce. Sometimes an official or a court favourite obtains an alienation of the state's demands on a township or group of townships; but the grant, even if declared to be perpetual, is usually treated as temporary, in the sense that it is liable to be resumed at the death of the grantee or at the demise of the crown. That being the normal conception in systems like that of the Moslems in Hindustan, the agriculturists—especially if they were Hindus—were *taillables et corvéables à merci.* It was Sher Shah who, first among these rulers, perceived the benefit that might be expected from leaving a definite margin between the state's demand and the expenses of cultivation. The determination of this margin, and the recognition of the person who should be secured in its enjoyment, formed the basis of the system which, under the name of 'settlement,' still prevails in most parts of India.

"A fixed standard of mensuration having been adopted, the land was surveyed. It was then classified, according as it was waste, fallow, or under crop. The last class was taken as the basis of assessment, that which produced cereals, vetches, or oil-seeds being assessed to pay one-third of the average gross produce to the state, the other two-thirds being left to the cultivators. This was a complete departure from the law of Islam, for it made no difference between the revenue raised from Moslems and that raised from unbelievers. Sher Shah's demand was in no case to be exceeded. It is very noticeable that Akbar added to his policy of union the equally important policy of continuity of system. He aimed at securing to the peasant the power of enjoying his property and profiting by the fruit of his labours. The needy husbandman was furnished with advances, repayable on easy terms. The assessments when once made were assessed for nineteen years; and after the twenty-fourth year of the reign, the aggregate collections of the past ten years having been added together and divided by ten, the future collections were made on the basis of this decennial average.

"Care was taken to provide easy means of complaint when undue collections were exacted and to punish severely the guilty exactors. The number of minor officials employed in realizing the recorded dues was diminished by one-half. The cultivators were to be made responsible, jointly as well as severally; the cultivators of fallow land were to be favoured for two years; advances of seed and money were to be made when necessary, arrears being remitted in the case of small holdings. Collectors were to make yearly reports on the conduct of their subordinates. Monthly returns were to be transmitted to the imperial exchequer. Special reports were to be sent up of any special calamities, hail, flood, or drought. The collectors were to see that the farmers got receipts for their payments, which were to be remitted four times in the year; at the end of that period no balance should be outstanding. Payments were if possible to be voluntary, but the standing crops were theoretically hypothecated, and where needful were to be attached. Above all, there was to be an accurate and minute record of each man's holding and liabilities. The very successful land-revenue system of British India is little more than a modification of these principles."

One special feature of Todar Mal's system was the enactment that all government accounts should be kept in Persian, instead of in Hindi, as heretofore. As Blochmann well says, "He thus forced his co-religionists to learn the court language of their rulers—a circumstance that may be compared with the introduction of the English language in the courts of India. The study of Persian therefore became necessary for its pecuniary advantage. Todar Mal's order, and Akbar's generous policy of allowing Hindus to compete for the highest honours—Man Singh was the first 'Commander of seven thousand'—explain two facts: first, that before the end of the eighteenth century the Hindus had almost become the Persian teachers of the Mohammedans; secondly, that a new dialect could arise in Upper India, the *Urdu*, which, without the Hindus as receiving medium, could never have been called into existence. Whether we attach more importance to Todar Mal's order or to Akbar's policy, which when once initiated his successors, willing or not, had to follow, one fact should be borne in mind—that before the time of Akbar the Hindus as a rule did not study Persian and stood therefore politically below their Mohammedan rulers."

Such changes, which put the subdued Hindu absolutely on a level with the conquering Moslem, were naturally repugnant to Akbar's more bigoted followers. The contemporary historian Badauni writes bitterly on the subject, and his cynicism is a useful corrective to the enthusiastic panegyrics of other writers of the time. Yet even when he wishes to make things appear in the worst light, he really shows the excellence of the intentions, at least, of the new measures, while exposing some of their defects. For instance, referring to one of the early attempts at land assessment, in 1574, he says:

"In this year an order was promulgated for improving the cultivation of the country and for bettering the condition of the *rayats*, or peasants. All the *parganas*, or fiscal unions of the country, whether dry or irrigated, in towns or hills, deserts or jungles, by rivers or reservoirs or wells, were to be measured, and every piece of land large enough to produce, when cultivated, one crore of tankas was to be divided off and placed under the charge of an officer called the *crori*, selected for his trustworthiness and without regard to his acquaintance with the revenue officials: so that in three years' time all the uncultivated land might be tilled, and the treasury be replenished. The measurement was begun near Fathpur, and one crore was named Adampur, another Sethpur, and so on after prophets and patriarchs. Rules were laid down, but were not properly observed, and much of the land was laid waste through the rapacity of the *croris*; the peasants' wives and children were sold and dispersed, and everything went to confusion. But the *croris* were brought to account by Raja Todar Mal, and many pious men died from severe beatings and the torture of rack and pincers. Indeed so many died after long imprisonment by the revenue officers that the executioner or headsman was forestalled."

All this is intended by the writer to cast ridicule on the reforms, but it really shows that they were good, and that they were, moreover, strictly enforced. The same cynic can see no advantage in Akbar's system of territorial commands. The Moghul officers, whether Hindus or Moslems, were spread over the land, and the state taxes were granted to them in certain districts (except the *Khalisa*, or exchequer lands) in return for military service. They had to bring a fixed number of men-at-arms, horses, and elephants into the field, and were rated, according to the number they brought, as *mansabdars* of ten, twenty, a hundred, a thousand, and the like. It was no invention of Akbar's, for we have seen it at work in much earlier times, and of course it was liable to abuse, though Akbar did much to remove the old dangers and corruptions of the system. Badauni said that the laziness, license, extravagance, and greed of the mansabdars ate up all the grant, and that no money was left to pay the soldiers, so the amirs dressed their grooms and servants as men-at-arms and passed them off at the muster, and then sent them back to their duties. "The treasure, tax-gathering, and expenditure of the mansabdars remained unchanged, but in every way dirt fell into the plate of the poor soldier, and he could not gird up his loins. Weavers, cotton-dressers, carpenters, and Hindu and Moslem chandlers would hire a charger, bring it to the muster, obtain a *mansab* [or order on the land-revenue], and become a *crori*, trooper, or substitute for some one: a few days later not a trace would be found of the hired horse, and they became footmen again. This sort of trade was carried on to a great extent [and Akbar knew it]; nevertheless the emperor's good luck was such that his foes were everywhere crushed, and soldiers were not so much wanted." As the enemies could not be crushed without soldiers, the system, though abused, appears to have answered its purpose.

There were doubtless many imperfections and many

cases of malversation in spite of Akbar's efforts; but this is only to say that the best system in the world is open to abuse, especially in an Oriental country, where to cheat the government is a virtue and to grind the faces of the poor a venial fault. The real reason that Badauni is so severe upon these reforms is that they were but a part of a general tendency to lax views on the part of the emperor. It was not merely in his just and equable treatment of the Hindus that Akbar showed his broad and open mind. There were other influences at work besides those of his Hindu wives and friends, and they all made for what the orthodox Badauni denounced as latitudinarian. A king who was constitutionally unable to see why a Hindu should pay more taxes than a Moslem was also liable to equally deplorable liberality in matters of faith, and Akbar had been deeply moved by the mystical doctrines of the Persian Sufis as revealed to him by two brilliant brothers. From the time when Faizi, the mystic poet, joined the emperor's suite at the siege of Chitor in 1568, and still more when seven years later he introduced his young brother, the gentle and enthusiastic scholar Abu-l-Fazl, Akbar's mind had been unsettled in religion. He was essentially eclectic, and saw good in almost every form of worship. From his youth he had delighted in the conversation of scholars and philosophers and had shown the greatest deference to real learning; he had books read aloud to him daily from his rich library, and would go through them again and again; and now under the influence of the speculative mind of Abu-l-Fazl—a man of wide culture and pure spiritual ideals, who recognized his hero in his king, and devoted himself to him with his whole heart—he began to encourage debates on doctrinal and philosophical questions and displayed an eager curiosity in the discussions.

These debates took place in a hall called the Hall

THE DIVAN-I-KHAS, FATHPUR-SIKRI.

of Worship (Ibadat-Khanah—supposed to be identical with that now known as the Divan-i-Khas), founded in 1574 at the city of Fathpur, which had become the emperor's favourite residence. The city itself was the offspring of faith. Akbar, at least in the earlier part of his reign, was a devout visitor of holy places, and frequented the tombs of Moslem saints. We read again and again how he made solemn pilgrimages to famous shrines; and one of his objects was to secure an heir, for up to the fourteenth year of his reign none of the sons born to him had lived. He repaired to a holy man dwelling in a cave at the village of Sikri, not far from Agra; the hermit promised him a son, and Akbar placed his wife, the Princess of Amber, under the care of the saint till her time should be accomplished. Sikri, as well as its local prophet, waxed rich and populous by the numerous visits of the anxious king. Palaces began to rise by 1569, and the prophet, Salim Chisti, set up a new monastery and a noble mosque. The aristocrats built them mansions near the palace. Sikri knew itself no more, and its name was changed to Fathpur, "the town of victory." Happily the seer was justified in the event, and Akbar's son, named Salim after the holy man, but better known as the Emperor Jahangir, was safely ushered into the world. Fathpur derived fresh lustre from this auspicious event, and Akbar lavished all the taste and art of the age upon its adornment.

Nothing sadder or more beautiful exists in India than this deserted city, the silent witness of a vanished dream. It still stands, with its circuit of seven miles, its seven bastioned gates, its wonderful palaces, peerless in all India for noble design and delicate adornment; its splendid mosque and pure marble shrine of the hermit saint; its carvings and paintings—stands as it stood in Akbar's time, but now a body without a soul. Reared with infinite thought and curious care, it was deserted fourteen years later. When William

Finch visited it five years after its founder's death he found it "ruinate, lying like a waste district, and very dangerous to pass through at night." Ruinate it has remained ever since, desolate and abandoned. No later ruler of India has ever aspired to dwell in Akbar's Versailles, just as none ever rose to the height of Akbar's ideals. In the empty palaces, the glorious mosque, the pure white tomb, the baths, the lake, at every turn we recognize some memory of the greatest of Indian emperors. We may even enter his bedroom, the Khwabgah, or "home of dreams," and see the very screens of beautiful stone tracery, the same Persian couplets, the identical ornament in gold and ultramarine on which Akbar feasted his eyes in the long sultry afternoons of the Indian plains. We may walk into the houses of Faizi and Abu-l-Fazl, the laureate and the premier of his empire, who sang his glory and chronicled his reign. We may stand in the audience-hall, with its pillar throne and galleries, where the keenest dialectic of Moslem schoolmen, Catholic priests, Pantheists, Zoroastrians, Brahmans, and Buddhists rose in heated battle for their creeds, till quarrels and coarse vituperation called up the bitter sneer of the puritanic Badauni and the regretful contempt of the royal seeker after truth.

Fathpur, with its beauty in desolation, has stirred the poetic vision of a Heber, and compelled the homage of the wisest critic of Indian art. Fergusson wrote of the "Turkish Sultana's House," which still overlooks the Pachisi Court where Akbar is said to have played his games of living chess with slave-girls as pieces moving on the checkered pavement, that nothing can be conceived so picturesque in outline, so richly and so marvellously carved, without one touch of extravagance or false taste. The five-storied Panch Mahal, a kind of Buddhist Vihara, and the house of Akbar's witty Hindu favourite, Raja Birbal, have their individual charm; while the frescoes in "Miraim's Kothi" are curious documents in the history of Indian painting, of which we obtain some glimpses in the albums of Moghul portraits, drawn by artists of the Panjab and now preserved in the British Museum and a few private collections. The presence of Jesuit Fathers at Agra, attracted by the liberal views of Akbar, accounts for some of the characteristics of these curious paintings. Aureoles and angels appear; a little later we find the Blessed Virgin represented in a kiosk of Jahangir; and scenes of Christian hagiography were favourite subjects with Moghul artists. The Annunciation is believed to be depicted in a fresco at Fathpur-Sikri, while another strongly resembles the fall of Adam. There are even traces of the work of Chinese artists in the Buddhist paintings in the "Home of Dreams." Indeed this Indian Pompeii, with its unique and never iterative designs, is a museum of exquisite æsthetic genius. Akbar's views on art were characteristic. One day he remarked to some friends: "There are many that hate painting, but such men I dislike. It appears to me as if a painter had quite peculiar means of recognizing God; for a painter, in sketching anything that has life, and in devising its limbs one after the other, must come to feel that he cannot bestow personality upon his work, and is thus forced to think of God, the giver of life, and will thus increase in knowledge." He had always been fond of painting, and kept a number of painters at court, whose work

"THE TURKISH SULTANA'S HOUSE," FATHPUR-SIKRI.

was displayed before him every week. "Hence the art flourishes," wrote Abu-l-Fazl, "and many painters have obtained great reputations, while masterpieces worthy of [the famous Persian court painter] Bahzad may be placed beside the wonderful works of the European painters who have attained world-wide fame. The minuteness in detail, the general finish, the boldness of execution, and the like, now observed in pictures, are incomparable." This was written in Akbar's lifetime, and it is noteworthy that the historian distinguishes the Hindu painters as the best among the hundred famous masters of the age, though he mentions some great artists from Persia.

In this fairy city Akbar's dream of a universal religion grew into definite shape. It was in the Hall of Worship that he sought wearily to elicit truth from the debates of professors. "The unity that had existed among the learned," says Blochmann, "disappeared in the very beginning; abuse took the place of argument, and the plainest rules of etiquette were, even in the presence of the emperor, forgotten. Akbar's doubts, instead of being cleared up, only increased; certain points of the Hanafi law, to which most Sunnis cling, were found to be better established by the dicta of lawyers belonging to the other three sects; and the moral character of the Prophet was next scrutinized and found wanting. Makhdum-al-mulk [the head of the ultra-bigoted orthodox party] wrote a spiteful pamphlet against Shaikh Abd-an-Nabi, the Sadr [or chancellor] of the empire, and the latter retorted by calling Makhdum a fool and cursing him. Abu-l-Fazl, upon whom Akbar from the beginning had fixed as the leader of his party, fanned the quarrels by skilfully shifting the disputes from one point to another." The heated discussions of the learned men whom he gathered on Thursday nights to defend the dogmas of their creeds only inspired him with compassion for the futility of their reasoning and contempt for the narrowness of their grasp. In Akbar's eyes there was truth in all faiths, but no one creed could hold the master-key of the infinite. As Abu-l-Fazl wrote:—

> "O God, in every temple I see those who see thee, and in every tongue that is spoken, thou art praised.
> Polytheism and Islam grope after thee.
> Each religion says, 'Thou art one, without equal.'
> Be it mosque, men murmur holy prayer; or church, the bells ring, for love of thee.
> Awhile I frequent the Christian cloister, anon the mosque:
> But thee only I seek from fane to fane.
> Thine elect know naught of heresy or orthodoxy, whereof neither stands behind the screen of thy truth.
> Heresy to the heretic — dogma to the orthodox —
> But the dust of the rose-petal belongs to the heart of the perfume-seller."

Tennyson has finely expressed Akbar's dream of a pure and universal faith:—

> "I can but lift the torch
> Of reason in the dusky cave of Life,
> And gaze on this great miracle, the World,
> Adoring That who made, and makes, and is,
> And is not, what I gaze on — all else Form,
> Ritual, varying with the tribes of men."

It had taken many years to develop this new religion of catholic comprehension. Akbar would often sit, in the first hour of dawn, on a stone in his palace court, watching the rising of the sun and meditating on the mystery of life. He was passing through a stage of earnest doubt. He listened eagerly to the words of the Christian fathers, to the Vedanta philosophy of ascetic yogis, and he must have known the Buddhist doctrine and the profound metaphysic of India. He had versions of the Sanskrit classics to be made for him and he ordered a translation to be made of the Gospels of Christ. Badauni, the Mohammedan writer, says:—"In the year 986 A. H. (1578 A. D.) the missionaries of Europe, who are called Padres, and whose chief pontiff, called Papa, promulgates his interpretations for the use of the people, and who issues mandates that even kings dare not disobey, brought their Gospel to the emperor's notice, advanced proofs of the Trinity, and affirmed the truth and spread abroad the knowledge of the religion of Jesus. The emperor ordered Prince Murad to learn a few lessons from the Gospel and to treat it with all due respect, and Shaikh Abu-l-Fazl was ordered to translate it. Instead of the prefatory *Bismillah*, the following ejaculation was enjoined: 'O thou whose name is Jesus Christ.'"

Islam no longer satisfied him, though his instinctive devoutness still took him on pilgrimages to Moslem shrines, and as late as the twenty-first year of his reign he was contemplating a journey to Mekka. But Islam was too narrow for his expanding soul. The outward symbols went; the Moslem shibboleth vanished from the coinage, and the ambiguous formula "Allahu Akbar," "God is most great" (or, as detractors construed it, "Akbar is God"), took its place. When Moslems met, instead of the customary *salam*, they were to say "Allahu Akbar," and the reply, "Jalla Jalaluh," "May his glory shine!" was construed as containing another suspicious reference to Akbar's surname, Jalal-ad-din. While plainly declaring that he pretended to no divine incarnation, such as the Shi'as acknowledge, the emperor assumed a wholly new position in relation to matters of faith. He found that the rigid Moslems of the court were always casting in his teeth some absolute authority, a book, a tradition, a decision of a canonical divine, and, like Henry VIII, he resolved to cut the ground from under them; he would himself be the head of the church, and there should be no Pope in India but Akbar.

His first assumption of the rôle of priest-king was unintentionally dramatic. Following the precedents of the caliphs of old, he stood before the people in the great mosque of Fathpur one Friday in 1580, and began to read the bidding prayer (*khutba*), into which Faizi had introduced these lines:

> "The Lord to me the Kingdom gave,
> He made me prudent, strong and brave,
> He guided me with right and ruth,
> Filling my heart with love of truth;
> No tongue of man can sum His State —
> Allahu Akbar! God is great."

But the emotion of the scene, the sight of the multitude, and the thought of his high office were too much for him. Akbar faltered and broke down, and the court preacher had to finish the prayer.

Soon afterwards Akbar promulgated a document which is unique in the history of the Mohammedan world. It was drawn up by the father of Faizi and Abu-l-Fazl, himself a Shi'a pantheist, and it was signed, sorely against their will, by the orthodox divines and lawyers of the court. It set forth in unmistakable terms that the authority of the just king was higher than that of a Mujtahid (or sublime doctor of the faith), and that, should a religious question arise regarding which the Mujtahids were at variance, the emperor's decision should be binding on the Moslems of India, and any opposition to the imperial decrees should involve the loss of goods and religion in this world, and ensure damnation in the world to come. In other words, Akbar's judgment was set above every legal and religious authority except the plain letter of the Koran. It was a promulgation of a doctrine of imperial infallibility.

After thus breaking sharply with the principles of Mohammedan tradition, Akbar went, as of old, on pilgrimage to a saint's tomb. Badauni smiled grimly and said "it was strange that his Majesty should have such faith in the good man of Ajmir while rejecting our Prophet, the foundation of everything, from whose skirt hundreds of thousands of first-class saints had sprung." With the same superstitious bent, oddly contrasting with his philosophic theory, Akbar is said to have varied the colours of his clothes in accordance with the regent planet of the day, to have muttered spells at night to subdue the sun to his will, to have prostrated himself publicly before the sun and the sacred fire, and to have made the whole court rise respectfully when the lamps were lighted. On the festival of the eighth day after the sun entered Virgo, the emperor came forth to the audience-chamber with his brow marked in Hindu fashion and with jewelled strings tied by Brahmans on his wrists to represent the sacred thread. He was not above charms and sortileges. He studied alchemy as well as astronomy, and is reported to have exhibited the gold he had professedly transmuted, and he took boundless interest in the tricks and miracles both of the Hindu ascetics, or yogis, and of the Moslem fakirs.

The truth is that Akbar was singularly sensitive to religious impressions of every kind, and that his new religion, the *Din-i-Ilahi*, or "divine faith," an eclectic pantheism, contained elements taken from very diverse creeds. While overthrowing nearly every ceremonial rule, whether of Islam or of Hinduism, and making almost all things lawful save excess, he took ideas from learned Brahmans as well as from Portuguese missionaries; he adopted the worship of the sun as the symbol of the Creator, and himself daily set the example of "adoring Him the Timeless in the flame that measures Time"; as the starting-point of his new Ilaḥi era he introduced the solar year which begins at the vernal equinox; he forbade cow-eating, in deference to Indians, and had himself ceremonially weighed in Hindu fashion on both his solar and his lunar birthday; he instituted the sacred fire adored of the Parsis, and encouraged the *hom* sacrifice of the Hindus in his palace. The new cult was cordially professed only by a small band of courtiers calling themselves "the elect," and including Faizi, Abu-l-Fazl, and other Persians, chiefly poets, as well as one Hindu, Birbal, but the rest, even of the court, remained indifferent, when not hostile. Some boldly refused to join the new faith, but the most part temporized for fear of losing favour. Of course an eclectic religion never takes hold of a people, and Akbar's curiously interesting hodgepodge of philosophy, mysticism, and nature-worship practically died with him; but the broad-minded sympathy which

DARUGHA PERSHAD'S HOUSE, FATHPUR-SIKRI.

inspired such a vision of catholicity left a lasting impress upon a land of warring creeds and tribes, and for a brief while created a nation where before there had been only factions.

With the promulgation of the emperor's infallibility the debates in the Hall of Worship came to an end; the leading bigots Makhdum and Abd-an-Nabi were sent to refresh their fanaticism at Mekka, and the pantheists under Abu-l-Fazl and his brother enjoyed a brief triumph. Both held high rank, but Faizi prized his office of poet-laureate above any political power, while Abu-l-Fazl became Divan, or Treasurer, of the Province of Delhi. These two brilliant and sympathetic brothers were now Akbar's chief intimates, and he found in their devotion more than compensation for the solitary elevation that is the inevitable fate of a reforming sovereign born centuries before the accepted time. Probably they encouraged him in the fancies and extravagances which somewhat marred his later life. One of these fancies was a belief that the religion of Islam would not survive its millennium, and that its collapse would be accompanied by the advent of the Mahdi, the Lord of the Age, in whom Akbar was easily induced to recognize himself. He ordered a "History of the Millennium" (*Tarikh-i-Alfi*) to be compiled by a company of scholars, including the reluctant Badauni, to put a seal, as it were, upon an extinct religion. The events of the thousand years of doomed Islam were related from a Shi'a point of view, and, to add to the confusion, the chronology was reckoned from the death of the Prophet instead of from his flight (Hijra).

This was an example of Akbar's love of innovation, and it is impossible to deny that he was fond of experiment and novelty for their own sake. "All good things must once have been new," he remarked, and accordingly he tested the novel habit of smoking tobacco, which was first introduced in India in his reign. As Dr. Holden has said, "He experimented in all departments, from religion to metallurgy," and some of his changes appear to have been dictated by mere whim and restless curiosity, rather than by reason and judgment. His experimental spirit was displayed in the way he endeavoured to ascertain the natural religion of the untaught child. He separated a score of hapless babies from their mothers, and shut them up in a house where none might speak to them, in order to see what faith they would evolve. After three or four years the children were let out, and they came forth —dumb! The emperor's experiments were not always wise.

Nevertheless, he had wise counsellors, and it was an age of great literary abundance. Faizi was one of the most exquisite poets India has ever produced, and Abu-l-Fazl's "Book of Akbar" (*Akbarnamah*), written in 1597, the third volume of which forms the celebrated *Ain-i-Akbari*, or "Acts of Akbar," will always retain its fascination as a minute record of the customs and institutions of the greatest age of the Moghul empire. As Col. H. S. Jarrett, one of its translators, has said, "it crystallizes and records in brief for all time the state of Hindu learning, and, besides its statistical utility, serves as an admirable treatise of reference on numerous branches of Brahmanical science and on the manners, beliefs, traditions, and indigenous lore, which for the most part still retain and will long continue their hold on the popular mind. Above all as a register of the fiscal areas, the revenue settlements, and changes introduced at various periods, the harvest returns, valuations and imposts throughout the provinces of the empire, its originality is as indisputable as its surpassing historical importance."

While Akbar was busy in enlarging the boundaries of faith, his material empire had not stood still. The conquests of Gujarat and Bengal, though requiring more than one repetition, had brought the empire to the normal limits of Hindustan. Kabul and the Afghan country, ruled by his disloyal brother Hakim, had repeatedly revolted; Badakhshan was finally lost in 1585, and the merry Raja Birbal fell in a disastrous attempt to coerce the wild Yusufzais in 1586. But after Hakim's death Kabul was pacified, and Kashmir was annexed in 1587, while in 1594 Kandahar was included in the empire. These were small changes, but more important conquests were attempted in the south. Again and again in Indian history we find in the Deccan the bane of Delhi kings. Nature never intended the same ruler to govern both sides of the Vindhya mountains, for people, character, and geographical conditions are dissimilar. Nevertheless, to conquer the Deccan has been the ambition of every great King of Delhi, and the attempt has always brought disaster. Akbar was not immune from the Deccan fever, but it seized him late in life. Up to the last decade of his reign his power had scarcely been felt south of the Satpura range, and although he had taken Burhanpur and made the rajas of Khandesh and Berar his tributaries as early as 1562, their tribute was intermittent and their fealty barely nominal.

A viceroy of the Deccan was eventually appointed

A Type of Indian Beauty.
From a Photograph.

to consolidate authority, but in the hands of the emperor's bibulous son Murad, and his equally intemperate successor, Prince Daniyal, the office became contemptible. Murad's incompetence to subdue open rebellion in Berar led to his recall and the appointment of Abu-l-Fazl to the command of the army which in 1599 resolutely set about the reconquest of the Deccan. Akbar himself arrived at the seat of war, and success soon followed. Ahmadnagar, formerly strenuously defended by the Princess Chand Bibi, had again fallen after six months' siege, and Asirgarh, the strongest fortress in Khandesh, opened its gate in 1600. An inscription on that glorious gateway, the Buland Darwazah at Fathpur, records how "His Majesty, King of Kings, Heaven of the court, Shadow of God, Jalal-ad-din Mohammad Akbar Padishah conquered the Kingdom of the South and Dandesh, which was heretofore Khandesh, in the Ilahi year 46, which is the year of the Hijra 1010. Having reached Fathpur he went on to Agra. Jesus (on whom be peace!) hath said: 'the world is a bridge; pass over it, but build no house there: he who hopeth for an hour may hope for eternity: the world is but an hour—spend it in devotion: the rest is unseen.'"

In these last sad years the great heart of the emperor was weighed down with grief. He had lost his beloved friend, the poet Faizi, in 1595, two of his own sons were sinking to their dishonoured deaths; the eldest, Salim, was little better and had shown flagrant insubordination. And now the closest of his friends, the inspirer of many of his best thoughts and acts, was to be sacrificed. Prince Salim, jealous of Abu-l-Fazl's influence and impatient of his censure, caused this upright and faithful servant of his father to be murdered on his return from the Deccan in 1602. It was the last and crowning sorrow, and Akbar never recovered from the shock. The quarrels and intrigues of his worthless family hastened the end. At an elephant fight there was a scene of jealous disputing in his presence; the weary king gave way to ungovernable fury, as he too often did in this stricken period of his decay, and was led away sick unto death. Round the bed of the dying Akbar the intrigues for the succession went on shamelessly, but at the last he received his only surviving son, Salim, and invested him with the sword of state. He died in October, 1605, the noblest king that ever ruled in India.

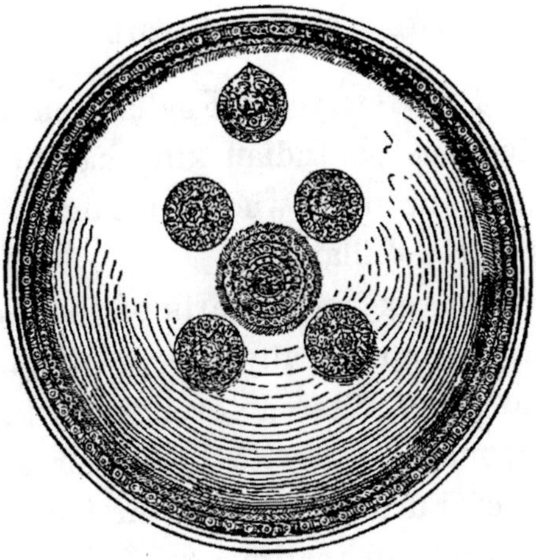

AN INDIAN SHIELD.

CHAPTER III

THE GREAT MOGHUL AND EUROPEAN TRAVELLERS

1605-1627 A. D.

TOWARD the close of the sixteenth century the curious began to listen to rumours, vague indeed, but impossible to be ignored, of a new and singular power that had arisen in the East. Stories were told of an emperor who had conquered the whole of Hindustan, and was ruling his vast dominions with extraordinary wisdom. Strange tales were bruited of his toleration. It was said that Christians were sure of a welcome at his court; that he had even taken a Christian to wife. Toleration was sufficiently out of tune with Tudor England, but in the barbarous East it possessed the charm of the wholly unexpected. The name and character of the Great Moghul became the common talk. In a few years Englishmen came to see him face to face, as no Indian king had been seen by Europeans since the days when Alexander met Porus on the plains of the Jihlam.

Hitherto, India, except in parts of the coasts of the peninsula, had been practically a *terra incognita*. What little was known had filtered through Portuguese missionaries, and one has only to turn over a few pages of the travels of Europeans in the first quarter of the seventeenth century to realize how little these writers were prepared for the sights they saw. They found a novel and almost undreamt of civilization, possessing elements of practical statesmanship and sagacity which the most philosophic of them all, the French physician Bernier, deemed worthy of commendation to the serious consideration of the minister of Louis XIV. They met with a series of spectacles, ceremonies, customs, religions, and systems of government which were wholly unforeseen; and where they expected to find at the utmost rude and vacuous pomp, they encountered literature and learning, poetry and art, and a reasoned theory of government, which, in spite of their Western prejudices, fairly compelled their admiration. With all this they discovered only too many examples of superstition and degradation, and witnessed scenes of savage cruelty contrasted with barbaric splendour; yet the splendour and the degradation were such as belong not to uncivilized races, but to the exuberance of a great empire.

The native annalists of the Moghul period are both

numerous and authoritative. No one who has studied the invaluable series of volumes in which the late Sir Henry Elliot and Professor Dowson epitomized the "History of India as told by its own Historians," and extracts from which are given in the fifth volume of the present series, will be disposed to depreciate the importance of the Persian chronicles therein rendered with such erudition and skill. But the native writers have serious defects. They are prone to panegyric and are disposed to exaggerate the merits of reigning sovereigns and contemporary magnates with the traditional obsequiency of the Oriental author. They are apt to suppress facts which tell against their hero, and it is rare to come across an Indian writer with the critical or historical faculty. Besides, they naturally assume a familiarity with the every-day customs and methods of the age in India which a Western reader does not possess. They write as Indians for Indians. Had we to depend entirely upon them, our insight into life in the Moghul empire in the seventeenth century would be shallow. Fortunately we have other witnesses. Europeans of various nations, qualified in many respects to observe with penetration and record with accuracy, visited India in the period of Moghul supremacy, and their observations complete and correct with singular minuteness the narratives of native chroniclers.

The Fates were unusually propitious when they ordained that the Saturnian Age of Moghul power should coincide with the new epoch in European intercourse with the East. Up to the closing years of the sixteenth century a single European nation had held the monopoly of commerce in the East Indies. When Vasco da Gama rounded the Cape of Good Hope and landed at Calicut in 1498, the trade with India and the Far East passed into a Portuguese channel. The old routes had been in the hands of Mohammedan traders, who shipped their goods by the Persian Gulf

A BUDGEROW, CALCUTTA.

and the Red Sea, and so overland to Syrian and Egyptian ports, whence the merchandise found its way to Europe in Venetian bottoms. These routes were tapped at their source when Portugal acquired the command of the Indian Ocean. In the hands of such heroes as Pacheco, Almeida, and Albuquerque, the control of Portugal over the whole of the commerce with the East Indies, Spice Islands, and China was assured. Arab traders and Egyptian navies sought in vain to oust the invaders of their ancient privileges. From the Cape of Good Hope to China the extended coast-line was armed with a chain of Portuguese fortresses, and no ship could sail without a Portuguese passport.

But the age of heroes for Portuguese India passed away, and there were still no signs of a consolidated Portuguese empire in the East. Albuquerque had dreamed of such an empire, in the spirit of a Dupleix or a Clive, and he had exhausted his little nation by the constant drain of colonization. His policy had not been continued, and an empire on Indian soil was abandoned in favour of fortified trading centres supported by the command of the Eastern seas. The forts remained, but no attempt at any more ambitious settlement was made; and should the command of the seas be lost, there was nothing to save the commerce of Portugal with the East. The Spanish annexation in 1580 was the death-blow to Portuguese enterprise in the Indies; but the corruption of the nobles themselves, who found their Capua in the tropical verdure of Old Goa, had already paved the way to ruin. In 1597 the Dutch appeared in the Indies, and a few years later they were joined by the English, upon the incorporation of the first East India Company on the 31st of December, 1600. Even as early as Pyrard de Laval's voyage in 1607 the Dutch had almost destroyed the Portuguese monopoly of commerce with the Far East; and as soon as the English founded their factory at Surat, the Indian trade began to be transferred from Portuguese to English bottoms. The naval victories of Best and Downton off Surat and in Swally Roads decided the command of the sea, and the Indian trade of Portugal practically came to an end.

The opening of English trade with India was followed by the arrival in the Moghul empire of European travellers, and the publication of their experiences. Two sea-captains, Hawkins and Herbert; Sir Thomas Roe, the ambassador; two clergymen, Terry and Ovington; Dr. Fryer, and Hedges, the Company's Agent and Governor, form a tolerably representative group of Englishmen, and there were many more, as may be seen in the recently edited correspondence of the East India Company's factors. France sent Pyrard, who did not get beyond the Portuguese settlements in India; but the travels of Tavernier, Thevenot, and Bernier are among our best authorities. Pietro della Valle was "a noble Roman," Mandelslo a gentleman of the court of the Duke of Holstein, Gemelli Careri a Neapolitan doctor, and Manucci a Venetian. In such a cloud of witnesses of varied ranks, professions, and nationalities, truth, divested of insular or continental prejudice, may surely be found. The body of information furnished by their journals, letters, and travels, is indeed of priceless value to the historian of India.

The visit of William Hawkins to the court of the Great Moghul at Agra was a memorable event in the history of British intercourse with India. He was the first Englishman ever received by the Emperor of Hindustan as the official representative of the King of England, and he obtained from the Great Moghul the first distinct acknowledgment of the rights of British commerce in India. Hawkins sailed with Sir Francis Drake on his voyage to the South Seas in 1577. Thirty years later, in 1607, he commanded the "Hector" for the East India Company on a voyage to Surat, charged with letters and presents from James I "to the princes and governors of Cambaya, on account of his experience and language." He arrived at the bar of Surat, August 24, 1608, and soon discovered that his credentials would have to be presented to a higher potentate than those of Cambay. After twenty days he obtained leave to land his cargo, and was told he must deliver the king's letter to the Great Moghul in person. Accordingly, he dismissed his vessel to trade with a new cargo to Bantam. The Portuguese, however, were not yet innocuous, and their ships captured the "Hector" as soon as she sailed. The Portuguese captain-major received Hawkins's remonstrances with contempt, and set to "vilely abusing his Maiestie, tearming him King of Fishermen, and of an Island of no import, and a —— for his Commission." To these ignominious expressions a Portuguese naval officer added that "these seas belonged unto the King of Portugall, and none ought to come here without his license." Such was the reception of the first envoy of England at the port of the Great Moghul.

Hawkins soon found that his troubles had only begun. Notwithstanding Akbar's administrative reforms, it is clear that the local authorities in Gujarat were oppressive and venal, and nothing could be done without a bribe. The governor pillaged the seaman's goods, paying only "such a price as his owne barbarous conscience afforded. He came to my house three times, sweeping me cleane of all things that were good." Matters came to such a pass that the traveller had to defend his house by force of arms, for Padre Pineiro offered the governor forty thousand "ryals of eight" if he would deliver up Hawkins to the Portuguese. At last, on February 1, 1608-9, he received a pass for his journey to Agra. At Burhanpur he saw the viceroy of the Deccan, who received him well, talked to him in Turkish (a language with which Hawkins was familiar) for three hours, of course accepted a present, and invested him with "two Clokes, one of fine Woolen and another of Cloth of Gold; giving mee his most kind letter of favour to the King, which avayled much. This done, he imbraced me, and so we departed." A guard of Pathans hardly sufficed to save the traveller from several attempts at assassination, or what he believed to be such (for one cannot but suspect that the gallant captain made the most of his perils), but at length, "after much labour, toyle, and many dangers," he arrived at Agra on April 16, 1609.

GOLD COINS OF JAHANGIR.

At this time Akbar had been dead nearly four years, and a very different personage sat on the throne. The Emperor Salim, entitled Jahangir, or "Grasper of the World," formed a striking contrast to his father, against whom he had more than once openly rebelled. Born under a superstitious spell, named after a wonder-working saint, petted and spoilt, the boy grew up wilful, indolent, and self-indulgent, too lazy and too indifferent to be either actively good or powerfully evil. He had instigated the murder of Akbar's trusted friend and minister, Abu-l-Fazl; he was possessed of a violent and arbitrary temper; and, like his wretched brothers, Murad and Daniyal, he was a notorious and habitual drunkard, although, unlike them, he could control himself when necessary. His image may be seen depicted on his coins, wine-cup in hand, with unblushing effrontery: it is of a piece with the astonishingly simple candour of his own memoirs. As he grew older he toned down somewhat, partly, he says, from a conviction that he was injuring his health, but chiefly, no doubt, under the influence of his beautiful and talented wife Nur Jahan, the "Light of the World."

When he ascended the throne in 1605, at the age of thirty-seven, his character, never wanting in a certain indolent good-nature, had mellowed. He had become less savage and more sober; by day he was the picture of temperance, at night he became exceeding "glorious." But what was done in the evening was entirely ignored in the morning, and any noble who ventured to approach the daily levees with the least odour of wine upon him was destined to certain and severe punishment. Jahangir carried his daylight sobriety so far as even to publish an edict against intemperance, and he emulated his far more contemptible "brother" James of Great Britain by writing a Persian counterblast against tobacco. In spite of his vices, which his fine constitution supported with little apparent injury almost to his sixtieth year, he was no fool; he possessed a shrewd intelligence, and he showed his good sense in carrying on the system of government and principle of toleration inaugurated by Akbar. He was not deficient in energy when war was afoot; he was essentially just when his passions were not thwarted; and he cultivated religious toleration with the easy-going indifference which was the key-note of his character. The son of an eclectic philosopher and a Rajput princess, he professed himself a Moslem, restored the Mohammedan formulas of faith which Akbar had abandoned on the coinage, and revived the Hijra chronology, although for regnal years and months he preserved the more convenient solar system. He followed his father, however, in his policy toward the Hindus, and was equally tolerant toward Christians. He allowed no persecution or badges of heresy, but welcomed the Jesuit father Corsi to his court, encouraged artists to adorn the imperial palaces with pictures and statues of Christian saints, and had two of his nephews baptized, doubtless for reasons of his own. He could be magnanimous and forgiving, when he was not angry. He even bestirred himself to redress the grievances of the people—witness his specious "Institutes"—and had a chain and bell attached to his room at the palace, so that all who wished to appeal to him might ring him up without running the gauntlet of the officials. But it is not on record that anybody was hardy enough to pull the bell.

William Hawkins was the first to set on record a portrait of this "talented drunkard," and very curious it is. It was a singular situation for a bluff sea-captain to find himself, in a strange land, called upon to meet a great emperor, about whom absolutely nothing was known in England. There was nothing to suggest the most distant dream that in two centuries and a half the slight introduction Hawkins was then effecting between England and India would culminate in the sovereignty of a British queen over the whole empire where the "Light of the World" and her imperial husband then reigned. The gift of prophecy would doubtless have added considerably to the sailor's feeling of responsibility. As it was, he was quickly put at his ease by the complaisant emperor. Jahangir was so eager to see this messenger from a new country that he scarcely gave him time to put on his "best attyre"; and so far from seeming annoyed at the poverty of his offering—for the governor of Surat had left him nothing but cloth for a present—the emperor "with a most kind and smiling countenance bade me most heartily welcome," reached down from the throne to receive his letter, and, having read it by the aid of an old Portuguese Jesuit (who did his best to prejudice him), promised "by God, that all what the King had there written he would grant and allow with all his heart, and more." Jahangir then took his visitor into the private audience-chamber, where they had a long conversation, and, on leaving, Hawkins was commanded to return every day. The language of the court was

Persian, though every one could speak Hindustani; but Jahangir and several of his ministers were also familiar with Turkish, the native tongue of Babar and his descendants, and this was the language in which the emperor conversed with Hawkins. "Both night and day, his delight was very much to talk with mee, both of the Affaires of England and other Countries."

The two evidently suited each other well. Hawkins would have felt constrained in the presence of Akbar, but it was impossible to regard his son—at least of an evening—in any other light than as a jovial and somewhat tipsy boon-fellow. Hawkins for his part was a simple honest sailor, a little inclined to bluster, but just the man to take the emperor in the right way, and not at all apt to be shocked at an extra allowance of grog. The result of the harmony between the two was that Hawkins acquired a footing in the court more intimate than was ever afterwards enjoyed by any European, and held it for years in spite of the strenuous opposition of the Jesuits. At one time Jahangir granted everything that the Englishman asked, "swearing by his Father's soule, that if I would remeyne with him, he would grant me articles for our Factorie to my heart's desire, and would never go from his word." He talked of sending an ambassador to England, and tried to induce Hawkins to make India his home, promising to make him a mansabdar, or officer of four hundred horse, with an allowance of £3,200 a year. He even admitted him within the red rails before the throne, where only the greatest nobles stood, and saluted him by the lofty title of "Inglis Khan": all of which mightily delighted the honest captain.

No wonder "the Portugalls were like madde Dogges." The English khan was universally envied; but he had to work hard for his glory. Jahangir gave him little liberty. Half of every twenty-four hours

PALACE OF JAHANGIR AT AGRA.

he served the emperor, by day and night, and he was obliged to marry an Armenian—a "white Mayden out of his Palace"—to cook his meals for him, for fear of poison being mixed with his food. His position was, moreover, extremely precarious. The commission for an English factory at Surat was first granted, and then, under pressure from the Portuguese viceroy, withdrawn. "Let the English come no more," said the emperor, weary of the squabble. But Hawkins knew the way to mend the matter, and on his giving Jahangir a fresh present, this order was rescinded: "so this time againe I was afloate." Then the Portuguese plied the emperor with bribes, and Hawkins fell out of favour. Nur Jahan reversed this state of things for the moment, but Hawkins found it impossible to pin the emperor to his promises, and retired from court in disgust on November 2, 1611. He sailed for Bantam in the following January in Sir Henry Middleton's fleet, and died a couple of years later on his voyage home.

Hawkins's intimacy with the Great Moghul gave him unrivalled opportunities for observation, but he was not an educated or penetrating observer. A good deal of his information is obviously based upon hearsay, but there is a large amount of first-hand evidence which no historian of Mohammedan India can afford to neglect. He describes the life-peers, or "men of Livings or Lordships" as he calls them, in their several ranks, from those "of the Fame of twelve thousand Horsemen" down to those of twenty horse, and says there were altogether three thousand in receipt of such grants. The army raised by these mansabdars amounted to three hundred thousand horsemen, who were maintained out of the income allowed to their rank. On their death, all their property went to the emperor, and "all the lands belong to him," but "commonly he dealeth well" with their children. The king's yearly income he estimated at fifty crores of rupees, or over fifty millions of pounds. The royal treasury contained an infinity of gold plate and jewels, including five hundred drinking-cups, some of which were made of "one piece of Ballace Ruby." The servants, gardeners, grooms, and others, attending upon the court, he estimated at thirty-six thousand. There were also twelve thousand elephants, three hundred of which were reserved exclusively for the emperor's use. The

A COMBAT WITH IRON CLAWS.

daily expenses of the court were fifty thousand rupees, besides thirty thousand for the harem; or, altogether, £9,000, which comes to three and a quarter millions a year.

Hawkins describes the emperor as far from popular with his subjects, "who stand greatly in fear of him," and ascribes this partly to his preference for Mohammedans over Rajputs for posts of honour and command, and partly to his innate cruelty. Jahangir took pleasure in seeing men executed or torn to pieces by his elephants, and the dangerous sport of elephant fights was his favourite spectacle on five days in the week. He was said to have killed his secretary with his own hand on mere suspicion, and to have flogged a man almost to death for breaking a dish. He delighted in combats between men and animals, and made an unarmed man fight with a lion till he was torn to shreds. At last the keepers contrived to tame fifteen young lions, who played before the king, "frisking betweene men's legs," and with these animals as opponents the combats became comparatively bloodless. All this cruelty, added to a rapacious and severe government, produced disaffection among his subjects. Thieves and outlaws infested the roads, and many rebellions broke out.

The daily life of the Emperor Jahangir was scarcely edifying. "About the breake of day, he is at his Beades, with his face turned to the westward in a private faire room," in which was "the picture of Our Lady and Christ, graven in stone." Then he showed himself to the people, who flocked to bid him good-morrow. Two hours of sleep ensued, then dinner, after which the emperor retired to the harem. At noon he again held public levee till three, and witnessed the elephant fights and other sports. The nobles at Agra all came and paid him homage, and he heard all causes and complaints. He then said his prayers, and had a meal of four or five sorts of well-dressed meats, of which "he eateth a bit to stay his stomach, drinking once of his stronge drinke. Then he cometh forth into a private roome, where none can come but such as himself nominateth (for two yeeres I was one of his attendants here). In this place he drinketh other five cupfuls, which is the portion that the Physicians alot him. This done he eateth opium, and then he ariseth, and being in the height of his drinke, he layeth him down to sleep, every man departing to his own home. And after he hath slept two houres they awake him, and bring his supper to him, at which time he is not able to feed himselfe; but it is thrust into his mouth by others, and this is about one of the clock; and then he sleepeth the rest of the night."

Such was Akbar's successor, and such the sovereign to whom Sir Thomas Roe presented his credentials as ambassador of the King of England in January, 1615. Roe had come to complete what Hawkins had only partly succeeded in effecting. The English agents and traders were still in a humiliating situation, subject to all kinds of indignities, possessing no recognized or valid rights, and obliged to sue and bribe for such slight facilities as they could win. Their chiefs, the agents of the East India Company, had brought scorn upon their nation by "kotowing" to the Moghul dignitaries, cringing to insult, and asserting no trace of dignity; and had even "suffered blowes of the porters, base Peons, and beene thrust out by them with much scorne by head and shoulders without seeking satisfaction."

Englishmen were flouted, robbed, arrested, and even whipped in the streets. It was evident that a different manner of man was needed to retrieve the indignity done to our name and honour. Sir Thomas Roe was invited by the directors, after much consideration and debate, to accept the task, and the choice was approved by King James, whose royal commission duly constituted, appointed, ordained, and deputed "the said Sir Thomas Rowe our true and undoubted Attorney, Procurator, Legate, and Ambassador" to that "high and mighty Monarch, the Greate Mogoar, King of the Orientall Indyes, of Condahy, of Chismer, and of Corason."

Roe was in every way an excellent choice. He combined the business capacity of the great merchant with the urbanity and address of the courtier. His grandfather was lord mayor of London, and the blood of the Greshams ran in his veins; but he was entered at Magdalen College, Oxford, belonged to the Middle Temple, had been esquire of the body to Queen Bess herself, and was on terms of affectionate intimacy with Prince Henry and his sister Elizabeth, the future "Rose of Bohemia." Not yet thirty-five, he had led a voyage of discovery to Guiana and explored the Orinoco; he had disputed in Latin with Dutch divines; he had even sat for Tamworth in the "Addled Parliament." The East India directors described him as "of a pregnant understanding, well spoken, learned, industrious, and of a comelie personage," and Mr. William Foster, the latest and best editor of his journal, justly adds that "his commanding presence and dignified bearing were useful qualifications for a mission to an Eastern court, while in the still more important matters of judgment and tact he was equally well equipped. Sprung from a noted City family, he combined the shrewdness, readiness of resource, and business ability which had raised his ancestors to fortune, with the culture and experience obtained by a varied training in most favourable circumstances."

More than all this, he was a true Elizabethan, with the gallant bravery, the passionate devotion to king and country, and the great-hearted fanaticism of his age. It was not the merchant's son, but the Elizabethan gentleman, who faced the Moghul prince as an equal, and told an insulting prime minister that "if his greatness were no more than his manners he durst not use me soe; that I was an Ambassador from a mighty and free Prince, and in that quality his better." When the governor of Surat tried slyly to carry out the odious practice, hitherto tamely allowed, of searching the persons of British subjects, in spite of Roe's claiming the absolute exemption of an ambassador's suite, there was a spirited scene: "Master Wallis breaking out came up after me and tould me this treachery; whereon I turnd my horse and with all speed rode backe to them, I confess too angry. When I came up, I layd my hand on my sword, and my men breake through and came about me. Then I asked what they entended by soe base treachery: I was free landed, and I would die soe, and if any of them durst touch any belonging to me, I bade him speake and shew himself. Then they desired me not to take yt in ill part: it was done in Frendship. I called for a Case of Pistolls, and hanging them at my saddle I replyed those were my Frendes, in them I would trust. It was a Custome to be usd to rouges and theeves and not to free men: I was resolved not to return to my Country with shame; I would rather dye there with Honor."

Roe was certainly no meek-tempered man. His journal is full of similar scenes. But he did well to be angry, and his defiant and punctilious assertion of his dignity as the mirror of his sovereign, his insistence upon every necessary point of courtesy, and his stately refusal to unbend a jot of his proud bearing, had their due effect. When he came to India, the English were very nearly on the point of being driven out of even their slight hold at Surat; the influence of the Portuguese at court threatened to oust the scanty merchant colony which, in deep humiliation, was unconsciously laying the foundations of an empire; the Moghul authorities were accustomed to treat the English as beggars to be spurned. All this was changed before he left. Despite the opposition of the prince, afterwards Shah Jahan, who almost ruled his father, and who, as governor of Surat, had the means of making his enmity felt; in spite of the intrigues of the empress, the prime minister, and the Jesuits, Roe not merely asserted his countrymen's rights, but won a series of important diplomatic victories. He compelled the court favourite to refund his illegal exactions, and "recovered all bribes, extortions, debts made and taken before my tyme till this day, or at least an honourable composition." His firmness and courage, combined with wary management, were too much for the cleverness of Father Corsi, and the Portuguese almost lost their influence. The emperor and his son were men fully capable of

HOUSE OF CARVED TEAK, SURAT.

measuring and admiring Roe's manly qualities; and his independence and dogged persistence, supported by natural dignity and courtliness, won from the Moghul authorities as much advantage as could at that time be expected.

The ambassador tried in vain to obtain a general

treaty, embodying articles resembling the capitulations granted in Turkey. Experience taught him that the time was not ripe for any such concession, and the Moghul emperor was too ignorant of foreign kingdoms to measure India with them. "Neyther will this overgrowne Eliphant," said Roe, "descend to Article or bynde himselfe reciprocally to any Prince upon terms of Equality, but only by way of favour admitt our stay." "You can never expect to trade here upon Capitulations that shall be permanent. Wee must serve the tyme." All he could obtain were firmans, or orders to the local authorities, sanctioning the English trade at Surat upon reasonably satisfactory terms. "You shall be sure of as much priviledge as any stranger," Jahangir promised, and he kept his word. The English factory at Surat was set on a sufficiently stable basis, and officially recognized by emperor and prince-governor.

Indeed, Roe was disposed to judge favourably of the Moghul authorities, considering their ignorance and the uncertainty of their official position. "All the Government dependes upon the present will," he wrote in 1618, "whose appetite only governs the lordes of the kingdome; but their Justice is generallie good to strangers; they are not rigorous, except in searching for thinges to please [*i. e.* presents and luxuries], and what trouble we have is for hope of them, and by our owne disorders." He noted the turbulence of the English crews and even of some of the factors, and warned the Company against a policy of aggression: "A war and trafique are incompatible. By my consent, you shall no way engage yourselves but at sea, wher you are like to gayne as often as to loose. It is the beggering of the Portugall, notwithstanding his many rich residences and territoryes, that hee keepes souldiers that spendes it; yet his garrisons are meane. He never profited by the Indyes since hee defended them. Observe this well. It hath beene also the error of the Dutch, who seeke Plantation heere by the sword. They have a woonderfull stocke, they proule in all Places, they Posses some of the best; yet ther dead Payes consume all the gayne. Lett this bee received as a rule that if you will Profitt, seeke it at Sea, and in quiett trade; for without controversy it is an error to affect Garrisons and Land warrs in India."

Roe's journal is perhaps better known than any similar work on India; but it is extremely limited in its scope. It deals almost exclusively with the court and the ambassador's audiences with the emperor, and with the political intrigues of the time, but of the state of the country it reveals little. As a record of court life, however, it forms an admirable complement to Hawkins' narrative. Sir Thomas was admitted to the king's privacy almost with the freedom which the seaman enjoyed. Indeed, Jahangir seemed to be unable to distinguish between an ambassador and a buccaneer, and entertained his excellency with a familiar joviality which severely tried the patience of the grave diplomatist. He made him sneeze with his "strong drink," to the delight of the assembled court, and then fell asleep in his cups, when the candles were immediately "popped out" and Sir Thomas "groppt" his way out in the dark. Jahangir especially piqued himself on his taste for art; pictures and statues, even of the Madonna, adorned his palace, and in the hall of audience were displayed pictures of "the King of England, the Queen, the Lady Elizabeth, the Countesse of Somerset and Salisbury, and of a Citizen's wife of London; below them, another of Sir Thomas Smith, Governour of the East-India Companie." When Roe showed him an English picture, he immediately had it copied by Indian artists, so that the owner could not tell which was the original, whereat the Great Moghul "was very merry and joyfull, and craked like a Northerne man." In his usual communicative mood of an evening, "with many passages of jests, mirth, and bragges concerning the Arts of his Country, hee fell to aske me questions, how often I drank a day, and how much, and what? what Beere was? how made? and whether I could make it here? In all which I satisfied his great demands of State."

The ambassador must have found the privy council room of an evening anything but a suitable place for business. One night he was summoned thither after he had got to bed, merely to show the Great Moghul a portrait. "When I came in I found him sitting cross-legd on a little Throne, all clad in Diamonds, Pearls, and Rubies, before him a table of Gold, in it about fiftie pieces of Gold plate, set all with stones, his Nobilitie about him in their best equipage, whom he commanded to drinke froliquely, several wines standing by in great

A Dancing Girl, or Bayadere

The nautch girls, or professional dancers in India, are sometimes spoken of in European writings as the Bayaderes, a term borrowed from the Portuguese, who thus designated them. They are frequently connected with the temples and called Devadasis, "Servants of the Gods," acting as handmaidens of the priests who minister in the shrines.

flagons. So drinking, and commanding others, his Majestie and all his Lords became the finest men I ever saw, of a thousand humours." At other times Jahangir waxed solemn and sentimental: "The good King fell to dispute of the Lawes of Moses, Jesus, and Mahomet, and in drinke was so kinde, that he turned to me and said: I am a king, you shall be welcome: Christians, Moores, Jewes, he medled not with their faith; they came all in love, and he would protect them from wrong, they lived under his safety, and none should oppresse them; and this often repeated, but in extreame drunkenesse, he fell to weeping and to divers passions, and so kept us till midnight." On another occasion the ambassador found him sharing the coarse meal of "a filthy beggar" — a holy fakir, no doubt — "taking him up in his armes, which no cleanly body durst, imbracing him, and three times laying his hand on his heart, calling him father": for superstition was a potent factor in this singular specimen of royalty.

Among the court festivals which Sir Thomas Roe witnessed, none was more curious than the process of weighing the Great Moghul. "The first of September was the King's Birth-day, and the solemnitie of his weighing, to which I went, and was carryed into a very large and beautiful Garden, the square within all water, on the sides flowres and trees, in the midst a Pinacle, where was prepared the scales, being hung in large tressels, and a crosse beame plated on with Gold thinne: the scales of massie Gold, the borders set with small stones, Rubies and Turkeys, the Chaines of Gold large and massie, but strengthened with silke Cords. Here attended the Nobilitie, all sitting about it on Carpets until the King came; who at last appeared clothed or rather loden with Diamonds, Rubies, Pearles, and other precious vanities, so great, so glorious; his Sword, Target, Throne to rest on, correspondent; his head, necke, breast, armes, above the elbows, at the wrists, his fingers every one, with at least two or three Rings; fettered with chaines, or dyalled Diamonds; Rubies as great as Wal-nuts, some greater; and Pearles such as mine eyes were amazed at. Suddenly he entered into the scales, sate like a woman on his legges, and there was put in against him many bagges to fit his weight, which were changed six times, and they say was silver, and that I understood his weight to be nine thousand rupias, which are almost one thousand pounds sterling: after with Gold and Jewels, and precious stones, but I saw none, it being in bagges might be Pibles; then against Cloth of Gold, Silk, Stuffes, Linen, Spices, and all sorts of goods, but I must believe for they were in fardles. Lastly against Meale, Butter, Corne, which is said to be given to the Banian."

One of the lights thrown by Roe's journal on the administration of the Moghul Empire is contained in his report of a conversation which he held with the "Viceroy of Patan," which shows the profits derived by the mansabdars, or life-peers, from their appanages: "As for his Government of Patan onely, he gave the King eleven Lackes of Rupias (the Rupia sterling is two shillings two pence), all other profits were his, wherein he had Regall authoritie to take what he list, which was esteemed at five thousand horse, the pay of every one at two hundred Rupias by the yeare, whereof he kept fifteene hundred, and was allowed the Surplusse as dead pay: besides the King gave him a Pension of one thousand Rupias a day, and some smaller governments. Yet he assured me there were divers had double his entertainment, and about twenty equall." This being translated means that the governor of Patna was an officer, or mansabdar, of the rank of five thousand horsemen, nominally, but was expected to maintain a force of only fifteen hundred, which cost him three hundred thousand rupees a year. Nevertheless, he drew from the imperial treasury at the rate of five thousand horse, or one million rupees, thus gaining seven hundred thousand profit, besides whatever he could sweat out of the taxes of the province which was farmed out to him, except for the one million one hundred thousand rupees which he had to pay as rent to the treasury. In other words, this official drew a fixed salary of nearly £80,000 a year, besides what he could make out of the taxes, and without reckoning the pension of one thousand rupees a day, which is probably a confused repetition of the three hundred thousand allowed for the troops. It was at any rate four times the pay of a British viceroy of India.

Roe had no easy time, what with the intrigues of the court, the vacillations of the emperor, and the hostility of the Dutch, for whom he always nourished an inveterate dislike. "They wrong you in all Parts, and grow to insufferable insolencies, and vse vs woorse than any braue enemie would or any other but vnthanckfull drunckards that wee haue releeued from Cheese and Cabbage, or rather from a Chayne with bread and water." In his solitude and harassments his great consolation was the sense of duty ungrudgingly performed, and he could write to his employers proudly, yet without boasting, "My sincerity toward you in all Actions is without spott; my Neglect of Priuat Gayne is without example, and my frugalitye beyond your expectation. I was neuer an ill husband of my Credit nor any trust committed to mee. My Patrimoniall vnthriftines only I feele and repent. I will bragg of no industrie nor successe. Judge mee by my Actions, Not by the fauour of an Infidel King, with whom yet I stand on such outward showes of Creditt as Neuer any stranger did." His "frugalitye" was indeed extraordinary. He kept up the embassy on about £250 a year; his own salary was only £600; and though the Company received him with twelve coaches at Tower Wharf, and voted him £1,500 for his services, he returned a poor man, and was thankful to accept another mission from the king, though it involved a second exile, this time to Constantinople. In those days it was an exception for a man in his position to refuse, as unworthy of his high office, the many opportunities for making money in India; but Thomas Roe was fashioned in a refined and exalted ideal of conduct, and his high principles and noble character stand clearly revealed in his writings.

We shall obtain no more familiar glimpses of the jocund court of Jahangir after Sir Thomas Roe's departure in 1618. The ambassador's chaplain, Edward Terry, in his "Voyage to the East Indies," adds little; nor is much to be learnt about the court, or even the country and government, from the travels of Pietro della Valle, who visited Surat, Ahmadabad, and Cambay in 1623, and then turned south to Goa. He gives an amusing

TOMB OF NUR JAHAN'S FATHER AT AGRA.

account of the sumptuous mode of life among the English merchants of Surat, but he has little to tell of the Moghul empire, and he did not see the capital. But of the famous empress, the "Seal of Womankind"(Muhr-i-Nisa), Nur Jahan—or, as she was then called, Nur Mahal—he has this notice: "He has one Wife, or Queen, whom he esteems and favours above all other Women; and his whole Empire is governed at this day by her counsel. She was born in India, but of Persian Race, and was formerly wife in India to another Persian Captain, who served the Moghul. After her husband's death, however, a fair opportunity being offered, as it falls out many times to some handsome young Widows, I know not how, Shah Selim had notice of her and fell in love with her. At length he determined to receive her for his lawful Wife above all the rest, and as such she commands and governs at this day in the King's Haram with supream authority; having cunningly removed out of the harem, either by marriage, or other handsome ways, all the other Women who might give her any jealousy; and having also made many alterations in the Court by deposing and displacing almost all the old Captains and Officers, and by advancing to dignities other new ones of her own creatures, and particularly those of her blood and alliance. This Queen is called at this day Nurmahal, which signifies 'Light of the Palace.'"

"By degrees," says Mohammad Hadi, the continuer of Jahangir's memoirs, "she became, in all but name, undisputed sovereign of the empire, and the king himself was a mere tool in her hands. He used to say that Nur Jahan Begam had been selected, and was wise enough, to conduct the affairs of state, and that he wanted only a bottle of wine and a piece of meat to keep himself merry. Nur Jahan won golden opinions from all people. She was liberal and just to all who begged her support. She was an asylum for all sufferers, and helpless girls were married at the expense of her private purse. She must have portioned above five hundred girls in her lifetime, and thousands were grateful for her generosity."

So great was the influence of this Persian princess that Jahangir joined her name with his own on the coinage, a conjunction unparalleled in the history of Mohammedan numismatics, although there is no real basis for the popular tradition that she issued the famous Zodiacal Mohrs when the emperor appointed her mistress of the mint for a single day. Her unlimited dominion over her husband, who loved her with a supreme devotion, is the more remarkable since she was no longer young when he married her in 1610, and Indian widows of thirty-four are usually widows indeed. This gifted woman, aided by her subtle brother, Asaf Khan, practically ruled the empire during the greater part of Jahangir's reign, much to his satisfaction; but although at first her influence kept him straight and benefited the empire, her overweening power, covetousness, and unscrupulous favouritism aroused bitter jealousies; and to the resulting intrigues were due the troubles that darkened the closing days of the self-indulgent emperor, the weakening of the old martial spirit of the Moghuls, the corruption and cupidity of the court, and the rebellion of Jahangir's son. His reign so far had been successful and curiously little disturbed. There had been hostilities with the rana of Udaipur, which were ended in 1614 by the military genius of Prince Khurram, the future Shah Jahan; and, in addition to temporary revolts in Bengal and elsewhere, there was the constant difficulty of maintaining a hold upon the Deccan provinces, where there was hard fighting with Malik Amber, the able vizir of the Nizam Shah. The boundaries of the empire remained much where they had been under Akbar, though Kandahar was lost to the Persian Shah in 1622 and was not recovered till it was betrayed to Shah Jahan in 1637. On the whole, the years were tranquil until the question of the succession excited rival interests.

Jahangir's eldest son, Prince Khusru, who seems to have been always on bad terms with his father, had openly rebelled in the early days of the reign, and on his defeat had been condemned to a lifelong but not severe captivity, while many of his followers were impaled by his infuriated father in the presence of the youth whom they had followed to the death. Khusru had by some quality or other acquired extraordinary popularity—as Roe's journal repeatedly indicates—and people compassionated his dreary fate, and even rose in open rebellion in his cause, with the like enthusiasm that others in Great Britain showed for Marie Stuart or Prince Charlie. He was believed to have been blinded by his father, but Della Valle explains that, though the eyelids were sewn up, the eyes were still uninjured when Jahangir caused them to be unripped, "so that he was not blinded, but saw again, and it was only a temporal penance." Sir Thomas Roe met him and found him an interesting mystery. The second son, Khurram, reckoned him an exceedingly dangerous factor in politics. What actually happened will never be known; but when Prince Khurram went to restore order in the Deccan in 1621, he insisted on taking his elder brother with him, and there the unfortunate Khusru died—of a fever, as was said, but such fevers sometimes happen very opportunely in the East.

Khurram, or Shah Jahan as he was already styled, now became more clearly marked than ever as the future emperor. He was the best general of his time, and had overcome the Rajputs of Udaipur and the many-headed foe in the Deccan. He was an able administrator and a cool, calculating statesman; yet he was intensely unpopular in those early days, however well he overcame the prejudice afterwards. Sir Thomas Roe found him cold and repellent, though always stately and magnificent. "I never saw so settled a countenance," he wrote, "nor any man keepe so constant a gravitie, never smiling, nor in face shewing any respect or difference of mien." There was nothing in common between Jahangir and this capable, self-contained son whom the father, depressed by his gravity, plaintively exhorted to take a little wine, "not to excess, but to promote good spirits;" and to Nur Jahan, who had formerly supported him, he became hateful, perhaps the more so since he had won her brother Asaf's favour by marrying his daughter, the lady of the Taj. Her aim was to induce her husband to name as successor his youngest son (by another wife), Shahriyar, a handsome fool who had married her daughter by her first marriage, and so to keep the dreaded Shah Jahan out of power. Jahangir himself, however, favoured his third son, Parviz, who could drink level with himself. The result was civil war. Shah Jahan, no longer impeded by an elder brother's claim, took the field against his father, but was defeated, and after an attempt at independent sovereignty in Bihar and Bengal in 1624, and a final resort to the protection of his old enemy, Malik Amber, in the Deccan, the rebel prince made his submission, surrendered his few remaining forts, and sent two of his sons, Dara and Aurangzib, as hostages to Agra.

Shah Jahan was now apparently helpless, and the imperious queen next sought to gain the command of the army. The general, Mahabat Khan, however, was not to be won over, and seeing that his own command, even his life, was at stake, he took the bold course of seizing the person of the emperor while he was separated from his guard when on the point of crossing the river Behat (the Hydaspes of the classical writers) on his way to subdue a rising at Kabul in 1626. The empress, far from daunted by this unexpected stratagem, lost not a whit of her splendid courage. She secretly escaped to the imperial guard and marshalled her husband's troops against the division of his captor, riding at the head of the army on her tall elephant, armed with bow and arrows. Mahabat's Rajputs had burned the bridge, but the empress was among the first to cross the ford and engage the enemy on the other side. The struggle is thus described by Elphinstone: "A scene of universal tumult and confusion ensued: the ford was choked with horses and elephants; some fell and were trampled under foot; others sank in the pools and were unable to regain the shore; and numbers plunged into the river and ran the chance of making good their passage or being swept away by the stream. The most furious assault was directed on Nur Jahan: her elephant was surrounded by a crowd of Rajputs; her guards were

TOMB OF JAHANGIR AT LAHORE.

overpowered and cut down at its feet; balls and arrows fell thick round her howdah, and one of the latter wounded the infant daughter of Shahriyar, who was seated in her lap. At length her driver was killed; and her elephant, having received a cut on the proboscis, dashed into the river and soon sank in deep water and was carried down the stream. After several plunges he swam out and reached the shore, where Nur Jahan was surrounded by her women, who came shrieking and lamenting, and found her howdah stained with blood, and herself busy in extracting the arrow and binding up the wound of the infant."

Open war had failed, and the brave woman resorted to other methods. She boldly entered the camp and for months shared her husband's captivity. By degrees her arts lulled to rest the watchful suspicions of the general; she won over some of the leading officers to her side; and finally the emperor found himself at liberty, with his faithful queen beside him and the army at his command. Mahabat Khan fled to Shah Jahan. The victory came too late, however, for Jahangir had scarcely restored order at Kabul and paid a visit to the happy vale of Kashmir, his favourite summer resort, when he was seized by a mortal sickness, and died in October, 1627, before he had attained his sixtieth year. There was now little use in opposing Shah Jahan, who had Mahabat Khan at his side and the full support of the army. The empress's brother, the minister Asaf Khan, joined the rising power, which he had always favoured, and Prince Shahriyar, who never had the smallest title to the throne, was defeated,

EMPRESS NUR JAHAN, THE WIFE OF JAHANGIR.

imprisoned, and killed. A temporary stop-gap, Dawar Bakhsh, son of Khusru, vanished as soon as Shah Jahan appeared from his distant exile in Sind. The great empress proudly retired into private life, wearing thenceforward the white robe of mourning for her queer, loving husband. She was held in honour, and drew a handsome pension; but she appeared no more in public, and maintained her rigid seclusion until in 1646 she was laid in her grave close beside the tomb of Jahangir at Lahore.

COIN OF JAHANGIR AND NUR JAHAN.
Struck at Agra, A. H. 1037 (A.D. 1627-8).

GOLD COIN OF SHAH JAHAN, A. H. 1066 (A. D. 1655-6).

CHAPTER IV

SHAH JAHAN

THE MAGNIFICENT

1628-1658 A. D.

LIKE his father, Prince Khurram, who ascended the throne as Shah Jahan in January, 1628, was the son of a Rajput princess, a daughter of the rana of Marwar, and had more Indian than Moghul blood in his veins. From what has been recorded of his previous history, as one "flattered by some, envied by others, loved by none," in Sir Thomas Roe's words, one is prepared to find a haughty, reserved man, wrapped in political intrigues, personally indifferent to creeds and scruples, and disposed to favour his mother's race. In every one of these respects Shah Jahan refutes prophecy. All his former cold severity seems to have melted when once he had made a clean sweep of his rivals, and after his accession the new emperor was the most accessible though the most stately of monarchs. He discontinued the obnoxious ceremonial of prostration before the throne, upon which Jahangir had laid great stress; and his unfailing kindness and benevolence, joined to a gracious publicity and display, endeared him to the people. He was the most popular of all the great Moghuls, though not specially the idol of the Hindus. There was a tinge of intolerance in his perfectly orthodox, if not very ardent, profession of Sunni Mohammedanism, and this slightly bigoted twist was encouraged by his ever-beloved wife, Arjumand Banu, known as Mumtaz-i-Mahal, "the elect of the palace," the mother of his fourteen children, whose exquisite monument, the Taj at Agra, still witnesses to her husband's devotion. Good Moslem as he was, Shah Jahan was a man of sound judgment and knowledge of the world, and he was the last king to dream of letting religion override statesmanship. Many of his generals were Hindus, and his great minister, Sa'd-Allah, though converted, was a Hindu by birth. Jesuit missionaries still laboured at Agra, where their tombstones may still be seen in the "Padre Santo," and where, as Bernier records, they had a large and very fair church, with a great steeple and bell, which might be heard all over the town in spite of the Moslem's prejudice against the devil's musical instrument. Nevertheless, this toleration did not extend to the Portuguese of Hugli, whose piracy led to their destruction in 1631, save such as were sent as prisoners to Agra, where the church was then partly destroyed in the temporary excitement of fanaticism.

The result of all the popularity and good statesmanship of Shah Jahan—for in his father-in-law Asaf Khan, and Mahabat (who died in 1634), and Ali Mardan he had counsellors as wise and upright even as Sa'd Allah—was a reign of extraordinary prosperity. The French traveller Tavernier writes of the gracious rule of the emperor that it resembled "that of a father over his children," and testifies to the firm administration of justice and the universal sense of security. A Hindu contemporary almost outshines the Moslem and Christian eulogists in extolling the equity of the government, the wise and generous treatment of the cultivators, the probity of the law-courts, and the honesty of the exchequer personally audited by this magnificent paragon of monarchs. There is, no doubt, exaggeration in these panegyrics. Shah Jahan knew how to tickle the imaginations of his subjects by gorgeous pageants and profuse expenditure, and he could be good-natured and generous when it did not interfere with his personal comfort. But he was too shrewd a man to pamper the people, and his expensive tastes demanded so much money that there must have been severe pressure on the taxpayers, who naturally had no voice in revising the eulogies of contemporary chroniclers.

That such was the case may be gathered from the observations of Mandelslo, who ranks quite as high, as an intelligent traveller, as the more famous Della Valle. He was a native of Mecklenburg, and was educated as a page at the court of the Duke of Holstein. When this potentate in 1633 despatched an embassy to "the Great Duke of Muscovy and the King of Persia," Johann

ENTRANCE GATE TO THE TAJ MAHAL, AGRA.

Albrecht von Mandelslo, then only nineteen, begged to be allowed to accompany the ambassadors and explore the distant countries to which they were accredited. He was attached to the embassy as a "Gentleman of the Chamber," and was even granted leave to pursue his travels further, when the ambassadors' business was accomplished. Accordingly, when their Excellencies the Sieurs Crusius and Brugman departed from Isfahan in the beginning of 1638, Mandelslo pushed on to India by way of Persepolis, Shiraz, and Gombroon, where he took sail in an English ship, the "Swan," three hundred tons, twenty-four guns, Master Honywood, bound for Surat, and after nineteen days' voyage made the port on the 25th of April. Mandelslo's travels in India—he afterwards went to China and Japan—were chiefly limited to the usual stay at Surat, and a journey through Ahmadabad to Agra and back by Lahore to Surat. Out of the eight months of his sojourn in the Moghul empire, five were spent at Surat, while his stay at Agra was unexpectedly brought to an end, apparently before he had been a month at the capital. Nevertheless, he found time to prepare a famous journal of his stay in India, which was edited, after its author's death, by the German Olearius—a Latinization of the very Teutonic Oelschläger—and then translated into French with many additional details, by Abraham de Wicquefort. This Gallic version was rendered, in its turn, into English by Davies in 1662, and from this quaint translation our extracts here are taken.

Like Della Valle, Mandelslo was much impressed with

the Dutch and English factories, or trading-posts, at Surat. "They have there their Lodges, their Storehouses, their Presidents, their Merchants, and their Secretaries, and indeed have made it one of the most eminent Cities for Traffick of all the East." This was just thirty years after Hawkins had vainly attempted to save one cargo from the clutches of the Moghul governor, and another from the Portuguese. The new companies had evidently lost no time in strengthening their position. "The English particularly have made it the main place of all their Trading into the Indies, and have established there a President, to whom the Secretaries of all the other Factories are oblig'd to give an accompt. He manages affairs with the assistance of twenty or twenty-four Merchants and Officers, and hath under his superintendency the Factory of Agra, where they have a Secretary accompanied by six persons; that of Ispahan, where they have a Secretary and seven or eight other Merchants, that of Mesulipatan, with fifteen; that of Cambay, with foure; that of Amadabat, with six; that of Brodra and Broitscheia, with foure; and that of Dabul with two persons; who are all oblig'd to come once a year to Suratta, there to give an accompt of their Administration to the President."

Mandelslo was treated by both Dutch and English with the princely hospitality which has ever been a tradition in India. He was met by a coach drawn by two white oxen, and heartily welcomed by the president, who begged him to stay with him five or six months and entertained him royally. "At dinner he kept a great

Table of about fifteen or sixteen dishes of meat, besides the Desert." The favourite rendezvous for the English colony was the president's "great open Gallery," where his friends enjoyed the sea-breezes of an evening. There was a fair garden outside the city where they all resorted on Sundays after sermon, and where on week-days Mandelslo made a small fortune by winning pistol-matches, "shooting at Butts." Sometimes they made a night of it over some bottles of sack; but Mandelslo was an exceedingly virtuous young man, and spoke no English—two effectual bars to excessive conviviality.

When he went into the interior, the same hospitable reception awaited him, not only at the hands of the European agents, but also of the Mohammedan merchants. Short as his stay was, the assistance of his hosts enabled him to make the most of his opportunities, and his native gift of observation stood him in good stead. A knowledge of Turkish appears to have served him well, as it did Hawkins. As he goes towards Agra we pick up hints which help us to understand the state of the provincial government under Shah Jahan. In spite of the testimony of other writers, travelling seems to have been anything but safe in Gujarat in 1638. The Rajputs—a kind of "High-waymen or Tories," as Jürgen Andersen, in 1646, calls them, according to Davies's translation—infested the roads, and travellers had to journey in company with large caravans, and even had occasion to fight for their lives. Andersen describes the governor of Ahmadabad as a "judicious, understanding man, but hasty, and so rigorous, that his government inclin'd somewhat to cruelty." The "somewhat" appears inadequate, when Andersen goes on to describe how, when some dancing girls refused to come and perform at his bidding, this "hasty" governor instantly had their heads cut off in the presence of a company which included the English and Dutch factors. "Assure yourselves, Gentlemen," said he, "that if I should not take this course, I should not long be Governour of Amadabat." "There is no King in Europe," our traveller adds, "hath so noble a Court as the Governour of Guzaratta, nor any that appears in public with greater magnificence. In his palace he is served as a King. He makes his advantages of all the Levies and Impositions which are made in his Government, so that in a short time he becomes Master of incredible wealth."

Mandelslo describes Agra in his day as the noblest city of Hindustan, and the one in which the Moghul most delighted; but it must be remembered that New Delhi was not then built. He says it was as much as a horseman could do to ride round the city in a day. "Its Streets are fair and spacious, and there are some of them Vaulted, which are above a quarter of a League in length, where the Merchants and Tradesmen have their Shops, distinguished by their Trades and the Merchandizes which are there sold; every Trade and every Merchant having a particular Street and Quarter assigned him." There were eighty caravansarais for foreign merchants, "most of them three Stories high, with very noble Lodgings, Store-houses, Vaults, and Stables belonging to them." He counted seventy great mosques, and estimated the number of public baths "or Hot-Houses" at above eight hundred, their tax bringing in a considerable revenue to the state. Both within and without the city he saw numerous palaces of the rajas and lords, and, chiefest of all, the imperial palace, fortified with a moat and drawbridge. The treasure there jealously guarded was estimated on credible authority at above fifteen hundred millions of crowns, or over £300,000,000. "This wealth," Mandelslo explains, "is more and more augmented every day, not so much out of the ordinary Revenue coming in from the great Kingdoms he hath (in regard that as his Ordinary Expence abates not anything of his Treasure; so is it seldome seen that he increases it, by ought remaining at the year's end of his Revenue) as by the presents which are made him, and the Escheats falling to him at the death of great Lords and Favourites, who make the Moghul Heir to what they had gotten by his favour; insomuch that the Children have no hope to enjoy ought of their Fathers Estates, either Reall or Personall. For the Moghul's Authority is such, and his Power so absolute, that the Estates of all his Subjects are at his disposal. There is no hereditary Dignity in all his country. That of Rasgi or Raja, which he bestows rather upon the accompt of Merit, than Birth, is Personall, as that of Chan in Persia, and is not deriv'd to Posterity, but by the recommendation of Vertue. Not that it is to be inferr'd hence, that the Moghul does exclude from Charges the Children of such as have done him good service; but he gives them lesser charges by which they may advance themselves to the Chiefest in the Kingdome, if either an extraordinary Vertue or the Princes Favour call them thereto."

Mandelslo also describes the daily levees of the emperor, his appearance in the gallery at sunrise, when

RHINOCEROS FIGHT.

From Rousselet's India.

the nobility "salute him with their Patschach Salamet," at noon when he comes to see the beasts fight, and at sunset; but it does not appear that the German traveller was personally received at court.

Agra was a very densely inhabited city at this time, "of such extent and so populous, that were there a necessity, there might be rais'd out of it two hundred thousand men able to bear Armes. There is no Nation in all the East but hath some commerce or other at this place; but most of the inhabitants are Mahumetans, and all the Merchandizes that are imported into it, or exported out of it, pay ten in the hundred." The muster of the Moghul army has often been a matter of dispute, but Mandelslo gives a detailed account of the force commanded by Shah Jahan in 1630, which numbered no less than 144,500 horse, besides elephants, camels, and the like. The soldiers were armed with bows and arrows, javelins or pikes, scimitars, and daggers, with a shield for defence. "They have no fire Armes with wheeles, nor yet Fire-locks but their Infantry are expert enough at the Musquet," a statement distinctly contradicted by Bernier, who says the musketeers were horribly afraid when their guns went off, and lived in dread of their beards catching fire. "They know nothing," adds Mandelslo, "of the distinction of Van-guard, main Battle, and Rear-guard, and understand neither Front nor File, nor make any Battalion, but fight confusedly without any Order. Their greatest strength consists in the Elephants, which carry on their backs certain Towers of Wood, wherein there are three or foure Harquebuses hanging by hooks, and as many men to order that Artillery. The Elephants serve them for a Trench, to oppose the first attempt of the Enemy; but it often comes to pass that the Artificial Fires, which are made use of to frighten these creatures, put them into such a disorder, that they doe much more mischief among those who brought them to the Field, then they do among the Enemies. They have abundance of Artillery, and some considerable great Pieces, and such as whereof it may be said, the invention of them is as ancient as that of ours. They also make Gun-Powder, but it is not fully so good as what is made in Europe. Their Armies do not march above five Cos [ten miles] a day, and when they encamp they take up so great a quantity of ground, that they exceed the compass of our greatest Cities."

In the *Itinerario* of Father Sebastian Manrique, the Augustinian missionary, published at Rome in 1649, we read that in 1640 the city of Agra stretched for six miles along the Jumna, and had a population of six hundred thousand, excluding strangers, who crowded thither. He mentions the Jesuit mission and church, and afterwards journeying to Lahore, where the emperor was then residing, he describes an interview with the prime minister, Asaf Khan, Nur Jahan's brother, to whom he was presented by a Portuguese Jesuit, Father da Castro. Asaf Khan dwelt in a splendid palace adorned with pictures, some of which illustrated the life of Saint John the Baptist. At a banquet at which the emperor himself was present, Father Sebastian was amazed at the sumptuous fare and also at the presence of ladies of rank unveiled. This was in 1641, and Asaf Khan died the same year, leaving an immense fortune, in spite of the quarter of a million sterling that his palace at Lahore cost him. But, as Roe remarked, he, like all the court, was "greedy of gifts." Manrique learned from Father da Castro that the architect of the famous Taj at Agra was Geronimo Verroneo, a Venetian, and this accounts for the difference between this dream in marble and other Moghul works. As the learned topographer and historian, Mr. Keene, has well said, "As a building and apart from its surroundings it cannot be pronounced to be an organic whole. No relation can be discovered among any of the dimensions; the outline of

THE TAJ MAHAL AT AGRA.

the dome does not express the inward form of the vault it covers; the disengaged towers at the four corners have no use or purpose, either apparent or real. The fenestrations give little shadow outside, no light within. Yet, masked by the modern garden, and consecrated by the repose of the whole scene—glittering, gleaming, distinguished—there is something about the Taj, as we now see it, which is perhaps unequalled by any building in the world for that mysterious fascination which we express by the single short word 'charm.'"

The Taj Mahal was finished in 1648, nearly eighteen years after the death of the queen, who was interred, meanwhile, in a tomb in the garden. Tavernier saw it, while it was being built, and says that twenty thousand workmen were continuously employed. Long before this the other buildings which Shah Jahan carried out at Agra were complete. The palaces in the Fort were erected between 1628 and 1637, the great Mosque in 1644-50, and the Moti' Masjid, or "Pearl Mosque," was completed in 1653. But the Taj was to be the supreme masterpiece dedicated to a supreme love, and there was to be no haste, but yet no rest, about its elaborate and stately growth.

Whatever the glories of Agra, the capital of Babar and Akbar enlarged and enriched by Shah Jahan, they were eclipsed by the splendour of the new city which the prince of Moghul builders laid out at Delhi. Agra is full of his noble works, but New Delhi, or Shahjahanabad as he named it and as it is still called, was his creation. It was begun about the time that Mandelslo was in India, and ten years later, in 1648, it was finished, when, according to all accounts, it must have been the most magnificent royal residence in the world. The learned French physician Bernier, the pupil of Gassendi and school-fellow of Molière, who lived at the court for many years in the succeeding reign of Aurangzib, has left a graphic description of the new capital, extracts from which will be found in the next chapter. Fergusson, the historian of architecture, said of the palace of Shahjahanabad that it was "the most magnificent in the East—perhaps in the world." The fort in which it stands is about a mile and a half in circuit, the massive walls rising sixty feet above the river, and higher still on the moated side toward the land. "Two barbicans, each 110 feet high, guard the main entrance on that side, two smaller gates opening on the side facing the Jumna. Within was a vast series of public and private halls and apartments, with a mosque, bath-house, and gardens; the whole permeated by a marble channel bringing in the bright and wholesome water of the canal." The great mosque dated 1658, the year of Shah Jahan's deposition, is described by Mr. Keene as "raised on a rocky basement, and has three domes, and two lofty towers each 130 feet high. Its outside area is fourteen hundred square yards, and the approach is up a flight of thirty-three steps. Three sides of the quadrangle are arcades or open cloisters, the fourth being the sanctum itself, 260 feet long, with a depth of ninety feet. The hall of worship is paved with black and white marble, marked out for 899 worshippers."

In the stately city Shah Jahan spent his luxurious old age, sometimes leaving it for a summer excursion to the lovely valleys of Kashmir, whither he would journey with a set of travelling tents so numerous and complete that they took two months to pitch at the successive stages of the royal route. His coronation anniversaries were observed with splendid extravagance, and he would then be weighed, according to Moghul custom, in scales against the precious metals; bowls of costly gems were poured over him, and all these riches, to the value of a million and a half, were ordered to be distributed among the people. The emperor and the court had reached a pitch of luxury that fostered

SHAH JAHAN'S PALACE AT AGRA.

effeminacy. In his youth and early manhood Prince Khurram had been a brave soldier, a brilliant general, a prudent counsellor, and a stern and resolute governor. As he grew old he abandoned all active pursuits, gave himself up more and more to pleasure, and suffered himself to be managed by his children. His adored wife, the lady of the Taj, had died in 1631, in giving birth to their fourteenth child, and Shah Jahan, essentially an affectionate "family man," while denying himself none of the pleasures of the zenana, became engrossed in his devotion to his eldest daughter, the Princess Begam, Jahan-Ara. He was still the benevolent and popular king that he had always been since his accession, but his strength of character was gone; he had become a mere pageant of royalty, given over to ease and the æsthetic delights of the eye and taste. Dryden has drawn the contrast in "Aureng-Zebe":

> "O! had he still that character maintain'd
> Of Valour which in blooming Youth he gain'd!
> He promised in his East a glorious Race;
> Now, sunk from his Meridian, sinks apace.
> But as the Sun, when he from Noon declines,
> And with abated heat less fiercely shines,
> Seems to grow milder as he goes away,
> Pleasing himself with the remains of Day:
> So he who in his Youth for Glory strove
> Would recompense his Age with Ease and Love."

The burden of state interfered with his enjoyment, and he sought to devolve his power upon his four sons, to each of whom he gave the viceroyalty of a distant province, in the hope of stilling their dangerous jealousies. The sceptre was falling from his hand, and he tried to secure peace by breaking it in pieces. It was a fatal policy. The fragments of the sceptre, like the rods of Pharaoh's sorcerers, turned into so many serpents, which strangled the remnant of his power, till the rod of Aurangzib swallowed up the rest, and with them the Peacock Throne itself.

The Deccan was the Dauphiné of the Moghul empire. It was there that Shah Jahan had mustered his strength to try conclusions with his father; and it was thence that Aurangzib drew his forces in the struggle which ended in his coronation. As the chief warlike events of Jahangir's reign centred round his son's career, so Shah Jahan's later wars were mainly fought by Aurangzib. History had shown that whoever could rule the Deccan was fit to be master of India. Shah Jahan had won his spurs in that never tranquil government. It will be remembered that Akbar had annexed Khandesh and a portion of Berar, but had not conquered any of the four kingdoms into which the Bahmanid empire of the Deccan had broken up. The Nizam Shahs of Ahmadnagar, the Adil Shahs of Bijapur, and the Kutb Shahs of Golkonda were still powerful, though the Barid Shahs of Bidar were no more. The Nizam Shahs, being nearest to the Moghul frontier, were the most obnoxious, and their able vizir, an Abyssinian named Malik Amber, repeatedly routed the imperial armies, recovered Ahmadnagar, which Shah Jahan's forces had temporarily held, and drove them back to Khandesh. Malik Amber's skilful tactics with light Maratha cavalry, afterwards so successful in the hands of the same people against Aurangzib, perpetually harassed the Moghul troops and wore them out, till it seemed as if the empire of Delhi must once more withdraw north of the dividing mountain range. It was then that Shah Jahan had shown his mettle. Arriving in the Deccan in 1616, he skilfully detached the King of Bijapur from the support of Amber, and soon brought the vizir to his knees; in a year's campaign Ahmadnagar was recovered, and Malik Amber became a tributary vassal. Then followed Shah Jahan's rebellion, disgrace, and flight, and the Deccan province was intrusted to his brother Parviz, who speedily drank himself to death, leaving the command to the general, Khan Jahan.

Throughout Shah Jahan's reign the Deccan had been constantly disturbed by wars and rebellions. Khan Jahan had revolted in 1629, only to be defeated and killed in Bandelkhand two years later; but his conciliatory policy towards the Deccan kings, to whom he sold Ahmadnagar in order to strengthen his power, had weakened the Moghul position. The campaigns of A'zam, Mahabat, and Asaf Khan did little to restore the lost prestige; but when Shah Jahan advanced in person in 1635, the King of Bijapur at length found himself outmatched, and in the following year consented to a peace by which he agreed to pay £200,000 to Delhi in annual tribute. The Nizam Shah's dominions were absorbed in the Moghul empire, and his dynasty extinguished. So matters remained for nearly twenty years, until Aurangzib became viceroy of the Deccan in 1655, and proved it once more to be the way that led to the steps of the throne. This third son of Shah Jahan, born in 1618, had already been governor of the Deccan in 1636 immediately after his father's successful campaign against Bijapur; but the youth of seventeen seems to have been more occupied with thoughts of the world to come than with the earth beneath his eyes. In 1643, when only twenty-four, he announced his intention of retiring from the world, and actually took up his abode in the wild regions of the Western Ghats, where he adopted the rigorous system of self-mortification which distinguished the fakir, or mendicant friar of Islam. The novelty of the experiment, however, soon faded away; the fakir grew heartily tired of his retreat; and the prince returned to carry out his notions of asceticism in a sphere where they were more creditable to his self-denial, and more operative upon the great world in which he was born to work.

It is true his first campaigns were unsuccessful. Ordered in 1647 to take command of the provinces of Balkh and Badakhshan beyond the Hindu Kush, recently conquered from the Uzbegs by Shah Jahan's generals, Aurangzib found the position untenable in face of the unceasing hostility of the indomitable hill tribes, and withdrew his forces with heavy loss. Nor were his efforts in 1649 and 1652 to recover Kandahar from the Persians, who had retaken it in 1648, more successful. Aurangzib had again to retreat discomfited, as his elder brother Dara did from a third attempt in 1653. These campaigns in Afghanistan and beyond the Hindu Kush are of no importance in the history of India, except as illustrating the extreme difficulty of holding the mountain provinces from a distant centre; but they were of the greatest service to Aurangzib. They put him in touch with the imperial army, and enabled him to prove his courage and tactics in the eyes of the best soldiers in the land. The generals learnt to appreciate him at his true value, and the men discovered that their prince was as cool and steady a leader as the best officer in India. He had gone over the mountains a reputed devotee, with no military record to give him prestige. He came back an approved general, a prince whose wisdom, endurance, coolness, and resolution had been tested and acclaimed in three arduous campaigns. The wars over the northwest

TOMBS OF THE KINGS AT GOLKONDA.

frontier had ended as such wars have often ended since, but they had done for Aurangzib what they did for Stewart and for Roberts: they placed their leader in the front rank of Indian generals.

The inevitable destiny of a prince who had displayed such ability was to govern the ever critical province of the Deccan. His arrival in 1655 was the sign for a vigorous "forward policy." Not only were the kings of Golkonda and Bijapur in possession of provinces which had once been part of the kingdom of Delhi, but they were Shi'a heretics, whom it was the duty of an orthodox Moslem to chastise. Aurangzib found an invaluable ally in Mir Jumla, a Persian of brilliant military genius, who in many campaigns, as vizir of Golkonda, had shown himself a very scourge of idolatry and a persecutor of Hindus. This talented and ambitious officer had fallen out with his king, and now threw himself upon the protection of the Moghul. Overjoyed at the pretext, Aurangzib marched upon Golkonda in 1656, and, but for urgent commands from his pacific father, would have added that kingdom then and there to the Moghul empire. Foiled on the very eve of victory, he sent Mir Jumla to Agra, where the crafty Persian so worked upon the cupidity of the old emperor, by describing the wealth of the decrepit southern kingdoms that were ready to fall like overripe fruit into his hands, and by presenting him with an earnest of the treasures to be amassed in the shape of the famous Koh-i-nur diamond, which, after a series of strange adventures, now reposes among the crown jewels of England, that Shah Jahan consented to an aggressive policy. Aurangzib, reinforced by Jumla, accordingly wrested Bidar from the King of Bijapur, occupied Kulbarga and Kaliani, and was on the point of conquering Bijapur itself, the capital of the Adil Shahs, when his father's alarming illness in 1657 summoned him to the north. Once more he was balked on the very eve of triumph.

Shah Jahan was believed to be dying. There was no law of succession, and each of the four sons prepared to fight for the throne. Shuja' was in the east, governor of Bengal; Aurangzib was south in the Deccan; and Murad Bakhsh was in the west, making merry in Gujarat. To Dara was assigned the government of Multan and Kabul; but he had become so necessary to his father that he deputed his functions to others, and himself remained at Delhi, attached to the king's person. Each of the princes behaved more like an independent sovereign than a lieutenant of the emperor. They had the command of rich revenues, which they devoted to the formation of large armies in preparation for the struggle which they knew to be inevitable.

Shah Shuja' was first in the field. He at once announced that his father had been poisoned by Dara; proclaimed himself emperor; engraved his name on the coinage of Bengal, and set out to march upon Agra. Almost at the same moment Murad Bakhsh caused coins to be struck at Ahmadabad and the prayer for the king to be recited in his own name, and displayed his lordly instinct by immediately assaulting the city of Surat and extorting six lacs of rupees from its luckless merchants. Aurangzib, in the Deccan, alone of the four brothers, assumed no royal function. Whatever his designs may have been, for the present he kept them to himself.

Dara lost no time in sending out the imperial armies to chastise Shuja' and Murad Bakhsh. The former was easily repulsed: Raja Jai Singh surprised him at his camp near Benares, and attacked before sunrise, while the careless *bon vivant* was yet heavy with wine. After a brief contest the rebels gave way, and the dazed prince, scarcely awake, hastily took to flight, abandoning his camp and treasure, artillery and ammunition. Meanwhile Aurangzib had made up his mind to join forces with his younger brother, Murad Bakhsh, and at the head of the Deccan army shortly met him near the Narbada. Towards the close of April, 1658, the combined forces came upon the royal army under the command of the Maharaja Jaswant Singh, on the opposite banks of the Narbada. Under a withering storm of arrows and javelins, Murad Bakhsh charged across the ford, followed by the whole strength of the Deccan, and crashed into the royal forces with an overwhelming shock. Kasim Khan and his Mohammedans fled from the field. The Rajputs fought desperately, till of their eight thousand men only six hundred remained. The wounded remnant sadly followed their chief back to his desert fastness in Marwar. There he was received with bitter scorn. His high-mettled wife shut the castle gates in his face, saying that a man so dishonoured should not enter her walls: "If he could not vanquish, he should die."

The Moghul capital was in an uproar. Dara, exasperated by the defeat, resolved to wipe out the disgrace, and led a magnificent array to the encounter. The lowest calculation estimates his army at one hundred thousand horse, twenty thousand foot, and eighty guns, but many were half-hearted in his cause. At the Chambal, Dara found that his brothers, making a circuit, had already crossed the river on the 2d of June. The two armies came in sight of each other on the 7th, at Samugarh, afterwards known as Fathabad, "the place of victory." For a day or more they remained observing one another. The heat was such as is known only on the plains of India. It was a true Agra summer, and the men were fainting and dying in their heavy armour. Early in the morning, Aurangzib marshalled his men. Keeping the command of the centre for himself, he placed Murad Bakhsh in the left wing, appointed Bahadur Khan to lead the right, and sent forward his own son, Mohammad, with the advance-guard to act with the artillery, which was, as usual, in the van. Dara meanwhile disposed his forces in a similar order. He placed his cannon in front, linked together by iron chains, so that the enemy's cavalry might not break through. Immediately behind the cannon, he ranged a line of light artillery-camels, mounting brass pieces worked on swivels and fired by the rider. Then came infantry armed with muskets. The mass of the army was composed, as usual, of cavalry armed with sabres, pikes, and arrows. The last was the favourite weapon of the Moghuls and Persians; the hand-pike being the special arm of the Rajputs. Khalil Allah Khan commanded the right, Rustam Khan the left, and Dara himself was with the centre.

The battle began, as Moghul battles always did, with an artillery engagement; cannon were fired; rockets or hand-grenades were thrown to excite a stampede among the enemy's horses and elephants, and then the infantry came into action with their clumsy matchlocks, while flights of arrows flew over their heads from the archers behind. Dara's advance-guard, under his son, Sipihr Shukoh, then charged and drove in Prince Mohammad's squadrons, and this advantage was immediately followed up by bringing the left wing to bear upon Aurangzib's right, which wavered and seemed on the point of breaking, when reinforcements came up opportunely from the centre. After this the engagement became general. Dara, towering high above his horsemen on a beautiful Ceylon elephant, led his centre against Aurangzib, carried the enemy's guns, after severe loss, and routed the camel corps and infantry. With the shock of horsemen against horsemen the real struggle began. No Moghul prince, as yet, knew the colour of the "white feather," and Dara displayed all the splendid valour of his famous blood. Emptying their quivers upon the Deccan horse, he and his men drew their swords, and fought hand to hand till the enemy began to break and fly.

It was the critical moment of the fight. The day was going against Aurangzib. The flower of his cavalry was driven back, and he was now standing, with scarcely a thousand men about him, awaiting Dara's onslaught. Never was cool courage put to a severer test; but Aurangzib's nerve was steel. "*Dili, Yarana*, Take heart, my friends," he cried. "*Khuda-he!* There is a God! What hope have we in flight? Know ye not where is our Deccan? *Khuda-he! Khuda-he!*" Thereupon, with a splendid self-control that comes only of bravery, he ordered the legs of his elephant to be chained together, to make retreat impossible. The mere order was enough to restore the ebbing courage of the few squadrons that still stood beside him.

Meanwhile Murad Bakhsh was hotly engaged with Dara's right, fighting like a lion and reeking with slaughter. Three thousand Uzbegs charged up to his ensanguined elephant, and arrows, spears, and battle-axes rained so thickly that the frightened animal turned to fly. The Moghul courage was again put to the test. The elephant's legs were quickly chained. Then Raja Ram Singh, of the valiant Rantela stock, came riding up with his Rajputs, insolently shouting, "Dost *thou* dispute the throne with Dara Shukoh?" and hurling his spear at the prince, tried to cut his elephant's girths. The Moghul, wounded as he was, and sore beset on all hands, cast his shield over his little son, who sat beside him in the howdah, and shot the raja dead. The fallen Rajputs, in yellow garb, and stained with their war-paint of turmeric, were heaped about the elephant's feet, and "made the ground like a field of saffron."

The cool courage of the one prince and the fiery valour of the other daunted Dara's division. Aurangzib and Murad Bakhsh were still perilously hemmed in by raving Rajputs maddened with *bang* (opium), and furious at the death of their chiefs, but it needed little to turn the balance of fortune either way. It was Dara's unlucky destiny always to turn it against himself. At this crisis he committed the most fatal error that an Indian commander could perpetrate. All the army looked to his tall elephant as to a standard of victory. Yet now, when the day seemed almost his own, he must needs dismount. Murad Bakhsh was still there on his gory elephant, with his howdah stuck as full of arrows as a porcupine with quills, grimly dealing blow for blow and shaft for shaft. Aurangzib towered high above a seething scrimmage of Rajputs. But where was Dara? It was though the sun had vanished in mid-heaven. A blind panic seized upon the all but victorious army, and every man fled for dear life. Once a panic has got hold of an Indian army, no power can save it. In one brief moment the tide had turned, and the all but vanquished became the victors. For a terrible moment Aurangzib had steadily maintained his seat on his besieged elephant, and his reward was the Peacock Throne. A little too soon Dara had dismounted, to be "numbered among the most miserable of princes," a fugitive and a vagabond in the earth. Then, and not till then, did Aurangzib descend from his elephant, and, prostrating himself on the bloody field, give thanks to God for this great and glorious victory.

The victory of Samugarh was the signal for all the world to come and tender their homage to Aurangzib, who remained on the field of his triumph, busily engaged night and day in negotiating with his father's amirs. They required little inducement to come over to the side of the rising man. The Raja Jai Singh, who commanded the army which had successfully repulsed Shuja' in Bengal, gave his adhesion to the future emperor. The Maharaja Jaswant Singh presently followed his example and tendered his fealty to the new power. Dara had already fled with a few hundred followers, and his father had sent money and five thousand horsemen to assist him. Aurangzib now turned

SHAH JAHAN.

his attention to his most dangerous rival, the still popular Shah Jahan.

The father tried to induce his son to visit him, but Aurangzib, suspecting a trap, sent his son Mohammad, who entered the fort of Agra on the 18th of June, overcame the guard, and turned the palace into a prison. Shah Jahan never left the castle during his seven remaining years of life. He was allowed every enjoyment that his sensuous nature demanded, loaded with presents, and supplied with such amusements as most entertained him. His daughter, the Begam Sahib, and all his numerous women, kept him company. Cooks skilfully ministered to his appetite, and dancers and singing-girls enlivened his senile revels. Like many another aged voluptuary, he became wondrously devout at times, and holy Mullas came and read the blessed Koran to him. Aurangzib granted him everything, in fact, except liberty. The two became partly reconciled, and the father bestowed his blessing and forgiveness on the son, but they never met. Shah Jahan died in 1666 at the age of seventy-six. The new emperor hastened to Agra to pay respect to his obsequies, and the body was laid in a tomb near the beautiful Taj which the late sovereign had set up in memory of his wife.

MUMTAZ-I-MAHAL, THE LADY OF THE TAJ.

The day after Shah Jahan had been safely locked up, Aurangzib entered Agra, seized Dara's house and

The Fort at Agra

This massive stronghold, with its high towers and battlements of red sandstone, surrounded by a deep moat to give it extra defensive strength, is a noble example of a Moghul fortress and one of the most imposing of the grand buildings at Agra.,

treasure (equivalent to some £19,125,000), and at once pursued his brother. Murad Bakhsh, who had been enjoying the honours of kingship, accompanied him with all the glory of mock sovereignty and twenty-six lacs of rupees in his money-bags. On the road Aurangzib found, or made, his boorish brother disgracefully drunk, and, protesting that such a violator of the law of Islam could never sit on the throne, threw him into chains on July 5th. That night he was secretly conveyed to the state prison in the island Salimgarh, opposite Delhi, where he was executed three years later.

The successful schemer led the combined forces in the footsteps of Dara, by forced marches, day and night, with his usual unflagging energy, living the life of a common soldier, and sleeping on the bare ground. His stoicism awed his followers; but Dara's own tendency to political suicide saved his brother trouble. To sum up many months of misfortune, Dara once more braved the army of Aurangzib in the hills near Ajmir, and, after four days' hard fighting, was again put to flight. With his wife and daughter and a few servants he made for Ahmadabad. The servants plundered his baggage and stole the jewels of the princesses, and, to crown his misery, when the fugitive at length reached the once friendly city, he found its gates closed against him. His wife died of hardship and misery, and he deprived himself of his scanty escort in order to send her body to be honourably interred at Lahore. At last, after few welcomes and many rejections, after bitter bereavement and weary wanderings, the crown prince and would-be

Emperor of India was betrayed into the hands of his enemy. He was paraded through the streets of Delhi dressed in the meanest clothes, on a wretched elephant, covered with filth; and the tumult which this barbarous humiliation stirred up among the people nearly amounted to a rebellion. "Everywhere," wrote Bernier, "I observed the people weeping and lamenting the fate of Dara in the most touching language: men, women, and children wailing as if some mighty calamity had happened to themselves." In face of such alarming sympathy Aurangzib resolved upon a speedy execution. A council was held; Dara was found to be an apostate and the friend of infidels; and on September 15, 1659, he was ordered to death. Many bewept his fate.

Meanwhile Shuja' was again in arms as viceroy in Bengal, and was pushing his way up the Ganges valley, but in vain. He was soon hunted away to Arakan, conveyed by Portuguese pirates, who at once robbed and saved him, in 1660. The last glimpse we get of him is pitiable; wounded and insulted, he fled over the mountains, with but one woman and three faithful followers, and was heard of no more. The last rival was accounted for, but Aurangzib had not waited for this. He had already twice assumed the throne: first hurriedly in the garden of Shalimar outside Delhi in the closing days of July, 1658, and then formally ascending it in state on the 26th of May, 1659.

CHAPTER V

THE PURITAN EMPEROR

AURANGZIB

1659-1680 A.D.

AURANGZIB took for his title the Persian word engraved on the sword which his captive father had given him—Alamgir, "World-compeller"—and by this title he was known to his subjects and to succeeding generations of Moslems. Before we consider the use he made of his power we must realize something of his character.

Aurangzib was, first and last, a stern Puritan. Nothing in life—neither throne, nor love, nor ease—weighed for an instant in his mind against his fealty to the principles of Islam. For religion he persecuted the Hindus and destroyed their temples, while he damaged his exchequer by abolishing the time-honoured tax on the religious festivals and fairs of the unbelievers. For religion's sake he waged his unending wars in the Deccan, not so much to stretch wider the boundaries of his great empire, as to bring the lands of the heretical Shi'a within the dominion of orthodox Islam. Religion induced Aurangzib to abjure the pleasures of the senses as completely as if he had indeed become the fakir he had once desired to be. No animal food passed his lips, and his drink was water; so that, as Tavernier says, he became "thin and meagre, to which the great fasts which he keeps have contributed. During the whole of the duration of the comet [four weeks, in 1665], which appeared very large in India, where I then was, Aurangzib drank only a little water and ate a small quantity of millet bread; this so much affected his health that he nearly died, for besides this he slept on the ground, with only a tiger-skin over him; and since that time he has never had perfect health." Following the Prophet's precept that every Moslem should practise a trade, he devoted his leisure to making skull-caps, which were doubtless bought up by the courtiers of Delhi with the same enthusiasm as was shown by the ladies of Moscow for Count Tolstoi's boots. He not only knew the Koran by heart, but copied it twice over in his fine calligraphy, and sent the manuscripts, richly adorned, as gifts to Mekka and Medina. Except the pilgrimage, which he dared not risk lest he should come back to find an occupied throne, he left nothing undone of the whole duty of the Moslem.

Aurangzib, it must be remembered, might have cast the precepts of Mohammed to the winds and still kept —nay, strengthened—his hold of the sceptre of Hindustan. After the general slaughter of his rivals, his seat on the Peacock Throne was as secure as ever had been Shah Jahan's or Jahangir's. They held their power in spite of flagrant violations of the law of Islam; they abandoned themselves to voluptuous ease, to "Wein, Weib, und Gesang," and still their empire held together; even Akbar, model of Indian sovereigns, owed

CAP MAKERS AND TURBAN FITTERS.

much of his success to his open disregard of the Mohammedan religion. The empire had been governed by men of the world, and their government had been good. There was nothing but his own conscience to prevent Aurangzib from adopting the eclectic philosophy of Akbar, the luxurious profligacy of Jahangir, or the splendid ease of Shah Jahan. The Hindus would have preferred anything to a Mohammedan bigot. The Rajput princes only wanted to be let alone. The Deccan would never have troubled Hindustan if Hindustan had not invaded it. Probably any other Moghul prince would have followed in the steps of the kings his fore-

HINDU MUSICIANS.

fathers, and emulated the indolence and vice of the luxurious court in which he had received his earliest impressions.

Aurangzib did none of these things. For the first time in their history the Moghuls beheld a rigid Moslem in their emperor—a Moslem as sternly repressive of himself as of the people around him, a king who was prepared to stake his throne for the sake of the faith. He must have known that compromise and conciliation formed the easiest and safest policy in an empire composed of heterogeneous elements of race and religion. He was no youthful enthusiast when he ascended the throne at Delhi, but a man of forty, deeply experienced in the policies and prejudices of the various sections of his subjects. He must have been fully conscious of the dangerous path he was pursuing, and well aware that to run a-tilt against every Hindu sentiment, to alienate his Persian adherents, the flower of his general staff, by deliberate opposition to their cherished ideas, and to disgust his nobles by suppressing the luxury of a jovial court, was to invite revolution. Yet he chose this course, and adhered to it with unbending resolve through close on fifty years of unchallenged sovereignty. The flame of religious zeal blazed as hotly in his soul when he lay dying among the ruins of his Grand Army of the Deccan, an old man on the verge of ninety, as when, in the same fatal province, then but a youth in the springtime of life, he had thrown off the purple of viceregal state and adopted the mean garb of a mendicant fakir.

All this he did out of no profound scheme of policy, but from sheer conviction of right. Aurangzib was born with an indomitable resolution. He had early formed his ideal of life, and every spring of his vigorous will was stretched at full tension in the effort to attain it. His was no ordinary courage. That he was physically brave is only to say he was a Moghul prince of the old lion-hearted stock. But he was among the bravest even in their valiant rank. In the crisis of the campaign in Balkh, when the enemy, "like locusts and ants," hemmed him in on every side, and steel was clashing all around him, the setting sun heralded the hour of evening prayer: Aurangzib, unmoved amid the din of battle, dismounted and bowed himself on the bare ground in the complicated ritual of Islam, as composedly as if he had been performing the *rik'a* (prostration) in the mosque at Agra. The king of the Uzbegs noted the action, and exclaimed, "To fight with such a man is self-destruction!"

We may read Aurangzib's ideal of enlightened kingship in his reply to one of the nobles who remonstrated with him on his incessant application to affairs of state: "I was sent into the world by Providence," he said, as Bernier records his words, "to live and labour, not for myself, but for others; it is my duty not to think of my own happiness, except so far as it is inseparably connected with the happiness of my people. It is the repose and prosperity of my subjects that it behooves me to consult; nor are these to be sacrificed to anything besides the demands of justice, the maintenance of the royal authority, and the security of the state. It was not without reason that our great Sa'di emphatically exclaimed, 'Cease to be Kings! Oh, cease to be Kings! Or determine that your dominions shall be governed only by yourselves.'" In the same spirit he wrote to Shah Jahan: "Almighty God bestows his trusts upon him who discharges the duty of cherishing his subjects and protecting the people. It is manifest and clear to the wise that a wolf is no fit shepherd, neither can a

AURANGZIB.

faint-hearted man carry out the great duty of government. Sovereignty is the guardianship of the people, not self-indulgence and profligacy." And these were not merely fine sentiments, but ruling principles. No act of injustice, according to the law of Islam, at least after his accession, has been proved against him. Ovington, who was informed by Aurangzib's least partial critics, the English merchants at Bombay and Surat, says that the Great Moghul is "the main ocean of justice. He generally determines with exact justice and equity; for there is no pleading of peerage or privilege before the emperor, but the meanest man is as soon heard by Aurangzib as the chief Omrah (amir), which makes the Omrahs very circumspect of their actions and punctual in their payments." Khalfi Khan, a native chronicler, tells us that the emperor was a mild and painstaking judge, easy of approach and gentle of manner; and the same character is given him by Doctor Careri, who was with him in the Deccan in 1695. So mild indeed was his rule that "throughout the imperial dominions no fear and dread of punishment remained in the hearts" of the provincial district officials, and the result was a state of corruption and misgovernment worse than had ever been known under the shrewd but kindly eye of Shah Jahan.

Yet his habit of mind did not lend itself to trusting his officials and ministers overmuch, whether they were efficient or corrupt. He was no believer in delegated authority; and the lessons in treachery which the history of his dynasty afforded, and in which he had himself borne a part during the war of succession, sank deep into a mind naturally prone to suspicion. That he lived in dread of poison is only what many

Moghul princes endured; he had, of course, a taster, and Ovington says that his physician had to "lead the way, take pill for pill, dose for dose," that the emperor might see their operation upon the body of the doctor before he ventured himself. His father had done the like before him. Like him, Aurangzib was served by a large staff of official reporters, who sent regular letters to keep the Great Moghul informed of all that went on in the most distant as well as the nearest districts. He treated his sons as he treated his nobles; imprisoned his eldest for life, and kept his second son in captivity for six years upon a mere suspicion of disloyalty. He had good reason to know the danger of a son's rebellion, but this general habit of distrust was fatal to his popularity. Good Moslems have often extolled his virtues; but the mass of his courtiers and officers lived in dread of arousing his suspicion, and, while they feared, resented his distrustful scrutiny. Aurangzib was universally respected, but he was never loved.

Simple of life and ascetic as he was by disposition, Aurangzib could not altogether do away with the pomp and ceremony of a court which had attained the pinnacle of splendour under his magnificent father. In private life it was possible to observe the rigid rules and practise the privations of a saint, but in public the emperor must conform to the precedents set by his royal ancestors from the days of Akbar, and hold his state with all the imposing majesty which had been so dear to Shah Jahan. A Great Moghul without gorgeous darbars, dazzling jewels, a glittering assemblage of armed and richly habited courtiers, and all the pageantry of royal state would have been inconceivable or contemptible to a people who had been accustomed for centuries to worship and delight in the glorious spectacle of an august monarch enthroned amid a blaze

THE JAMI' MASJID, OR GREAT MOSQUE AT DELHI.

of splendour. Among Orientals especially the clothes make the king.

The emperor divided his residence between Delhi and Agra, but Delhi was the chief capital, where most of the state ceremonies took place. Agra had been the metropolis of Akbar, and usually of Jahangir, but its sultry climate interfered with the enjoyment of their luxurious successor, and the court was accordingly removed, at least for a large part of the year, to New Delhi, the "City of Shah Jahan." The ruins of this splendid capital, its mosques, and the noble remains of its superb palace are familiar to every reader. To see it as it was in its glory, however, we must look through the eyes of Bernier, who saw it when only eleven years had passed since its completion. His description was written at the capital itself in 1663, after he had spent four years of continuous residence there; so we have every reason to assume that he knew his Delhi thoroughly.

The city, he tells us, was built in the form of a crescent on the right bank of the Jumna, which formed its northeastern boundary, and was crossed by a single bridge of boats. The flat surrounding country was then, as now, richly wooded and cultivated, and the city was famous for its luxuriant gardens. The circuit of the walls was six or seven miles, but outside the gates were extensive suburbs, where the chief nobles and wealthy merchants had their luxurious houses; and there also were the decayed and straggling remains of the older city just without the walls of its supplanter. Numberless narrow streets intersected this wide area and displayed every variety of building, from the thatched mud and bamboo huts of the troopers and camp-followers, and the clay or brick houses of the smaller officials and merchants, to the spacious mansions of the chief nobles, with their courtyards and gardens, fountains and cool matted chambers, open to the four winds, where the afternoon siesta might be enjoyed during the heats. Two main streets, perhaps thirty paces wide and very long and straight, lined with covered arcades of shops, led into the "great royal square" which fronted the fortress, or palace of the emperor. This square was the meeting-place of the citizens and the army, and the scene of varied spectacles. Here the Rajput rajas pitched their tents when it was their duty to mount guard; for Rajputs never consented to be cooped up within Moghul walls. Beyond was the fortress, which contained the emperor's palace and *mahal*, or seraglio, and commanded a view of the river across the sandy tract where the elephant fights took place and the rajas' troops paraded. The lofty walls were slightly fortified with battlements and towers, and surrounded by a moat, and small field-pieces were pointed upon the town from the embrasures. The palace within was the most magnificent building of its kind in the East, and the private rooms or *mahal* alone covered more than twice the space of any European palace. Streets opened in every direction, and here and there were seen the merchants' caravanserais and the great workshops where the artisans employed by the emperor and the nobles plied their hereditary crafts of embroidery, silver and gold smithery, gun-making, lacquer-work, painting, turning, and other arts.

Delhi was famous for its skill in the arts and crafts. It was only under royal or aristocratic patronage that the artist flourished; elsewhere the artisan was at the mercy of his temporary employer, who paid him as he chose. The Moghul emperors displayed a laudable appreciation of the fine arts, which they employed with lavish hands in the decoration of their palaces. A large number of exquisite miniatures, or paintings on paper designed to illustrate manuscripts or to form royal portrait-albums, have come down to us from the sixteenth and seventeenth centuries. The technique and detail are admirable, and the colouring and lights often astonishingly skilful. They include portraits of the emperors, princes, and chief nobles which display unusual power in the delineation of individual countenances, and there are landscapes which are happily conceived and brilliantly executed. There is no doubt that the Jesuit missions at Agra and other cities of Hindustan brought Western ideas to bear upon the development of Indian painting. Jahangir, who was, by his own account, "very fond of pictures and an excellent judge of them," is recorded to have had a picture of the Madonna behind a curtain, and this picture is represented in a contemporary painting which has fortunately been preserved. Tavernier saw on a gate outside Agra a representation of Jahangir's tomb "carved with a great black pall with many torches of white wax, and two Jesuit Fathers at the end," and adds that Shah Jahan allowed this to remain because "his father and himself had learnt from the Jesuits some principles of mathematics and astrology." The Augustinian Manrique, who came to inspect the Jesuit missions in the time of Shah Jahan, found, as we have seen, the prime minister, Asaf Khan, at Lahore in a palace decorated with pictures of Christian saints. In most Moghul portraits, the head of the emperor is surrounded by an aureole or nimbus, and many other features in the schools of painting at Agra and Delhi

LATTICE IN BATHROOM OF SHAH JAHAN'S PALACE AT DELHI.

remind one of contemporary Italian art. The artists were held in high favour at court, as we may judge from contemporary native accounts in which art is alluded to, and many of their names have been preserved. Their works added notably to the decoration

The Audience-Hall, Divan-i Aam, at Delhi.
From a Photograph.

of the splendid and elaborate palaces which are among the most durable memorials of the period.

The scene in the Hall of Audience on any great occasion was almost impressive enough to justify the inscription on the gateway: "If there be a Heaven upon earth, it is here, it is here." The emperor's approach was heralded by the shrill piping of the hautboys and clashing of cymbals from the band-gallery over the great gate, and Bernier thus describes the scene:—

"The king appeared, in the most magnificent attire, seated upon his throne at the end of the great hall. His vest was of white and delicately flowered satin, with a silk and gold embroidery of the finest texture. The turban of gold cloth had an aigrette whose base was composed of diamonds of an extraordinary size and value, besides an Oriental topaz which may be pronounced unparalleled, exhibiting a lustre like the sun. A necklace of immense pearls suspended from his neck reached to his stomach. The throne was supported by six massy feet, said to be of solid gold, sprinkled over with rubies, emeralds, and diamonds. It was constructed by Shah Jahan for the purpose of displaying the immense quantity of precious stones accumulated successively in the treasury from the spoils of ancient rajas and Patans, and the annual presents to the monarch which every Omrah is bound to make on certain festivals. At the foot of the throne were assembled all the Omrahs, in splendid apparel, upon a platform surrounded by a silver railing and covered by a spacious canopy of brocade with deep fringes of gold. The pillars of the hall were hung with brocades of a gold ground, and flowered satin canopies were raised over the whole expanse of the extensive apartment, fastened with red silken cords from which were suspended large tassels of silk and gold. The floor was covered entirely with carpets of the richest silk, of immense length and breadth. A tent, called the *aspak*, was pitched outside [in the court], larger than the hall, to which it was joined at the top. It spread over half the court, and was completely enclosed by a great balustrade, covered with plates of silver. Its supporters were pillars overlaid with silver, three of which were as thick and as high as the mast of a barque, the others smaller. The outside of this magnificent tent was red, and the inside lined with elegant Masulipatan chintzes, figured expressly for that very purpose with flowers so natural and colours so vivid that the tent seemed to be encompassed with real parterres. As to the arcade galleries round the court, every Omrah had received orders to decorate one of them at his own expense, and there appeared a spirit of emulation as to who should best acquit himself to the monarch's satisfaction. Consequently all the arcades and galleries were covered from top to bottom with brocade, and the pavement with rich carpets."

On his birthday Aurangzib maintained the old Moghul custom of being solemnly weighed in a pair of gold scales against precious metals and stones and food, when the nobles one and all came with offerings of jewels and gold, sometimes to the value of £2,000,000. The festivals often ended with the national sport, an elephant-fight. Two elephants charged each other over an earth wall, which they soon demolished; their skulls met with a tremendous shock, and tusks and trunks were vigorously plied, till at length one was overcome by the other, when the victor was separated from his

AN ELEPHANT FIGHT AT JAIPUR.

prostrate adversary by an explosion of fireworks between them. In the jovial days of Jahangir and Shah Jahan, fair Nautch girls used to play a prominent part in the court festivities, and would keep the jolly emperors awake half the night with their voluptuous dances and agile antics; but Aurangzib was "unco guid" and would as soon tolerate idolatry as a Nautch.

Indeed even his wives played but a small part in his life. According to Manucci, the chief wife was a Rajput princess, and became the mother of Mohammad and Mu'azzam, besides a daughter. A Persian lady was the mother of A'zam and Akbar and two daughters. The nationality of the third, by whom the emperor had one daughter, is not recorded. Udaipuri, the mother of his youngest son, Kam Bakhsh, was a Christian from Georgia, and had been purchased by Dara, on whose execution she passed to the harem of Aurangzib.

Even on every-day occasions, when there were no festivals in progress, the Hall of Audience presented an animated appearance. Not a day passed but the emperor held his levee from the window of the *jharukha*, while the bevy of nobles stood beneath and the common crowd surged in the court to lay their grievances and suits before the imperial judge. The ordinary levee lasted a couple of hours, and during this time the royal stud was brought from the stables opening out of the court and passed in review before the emperor, so many each day; and the household elephants, washed, and painted black, with two red streaks on their foreheads, came in their embroidered caparisons and silver chains and bells, to be inspected by their master, and at the prick and voice of their riders saluted the emperor with their trunks and trumpeted their *taslim*, or homage.

These gorgeous functions had little interest for Aurangzib. The art of government was his real passion. Of course, with his mixed and jarring population of Hindus, Rajputs, Patans, and Persians, to say nothing of opponents in the Deccan, his first necessity was a standing army. He could indeed rely upon the friendly rajas to take the field with their gallant followers against the Shi'a kingdom in the Deccan or in Afghanistan, and even against their fellow Rajputs, when the imperial cause happened to coincide with their private feuds. He could trust the Persian officers in a conflict with Patans or Hindus, though never against their Shi'a co-religionists in the Deccan. But he needed a force devoted to himself alone, a body of retainers who looked to him for rank and wealth, and even for the bare means of subsistence. This he found in the species of feudal system which had been inaugurated by Akbar. He endeavoured to bind to his personal interest a body of adventurers, generally of low descent, who derived their power and affluence solely from their sovereign, who raised them to dignity or degraded them to obscurity according to his own pleasure and caprice.

The writings of European travellers are full of reference to these amirs, or "nobles," as they call them, though it must not be forgotten that the nobility was purely official, and had no necessary connection with birth or hereditary estates. In Bernier's time there were always twenty-five or thirty of the highest amirs at the court, drawing salaries estimated at the rate of one thousand to twelve thousand horse. The number in the provinces is not stated, but must have been large, besides innumerable petty vassals of less than a thousand horse, of whom there were never less than two or three hundred at court. The troopers who formed the following of the amirs and mansabdars were entitled to the pay of twenty-five rupees a month for each horse, but did not always get it from their masters. Two horses to a man formed the usual allowance, for a one-horsed trooper was regarded as little better than a one-legged man. The cavalry arm supplied by the amirs and lesser vassals and their retainers formed the chief part of the Moghul standing army, and, including the troops of the Rajput rajas, who were also in receipt of an imperial subsidy, amounted in effective strength to more than two hundred thousand in Bernier's time (1659-66), of whom perhaps forty thousand were about the emperor's person. The regular infantry was of small account; the musketeers could only fire decently when squatting on the ground and resting their muskets on a kind of wooden fork that hangs to them, and were terribly afraid of burning their beards or bursting their guns. There were about fifty thousand of this arm about the court, besides a large number in the provinces; but the hordes of camp-followers, sutlers, grooms, traders, and servants, who always hung about the army, and were often absurdly reckoned as part of its effective strength, gave the impression of an infantry force of two or three hundred thousand men. There was also a small park of artillery, consisting partly of heavy guns, and partly of lighter pieces mounted on camels.

The emperor kept the control of the army and nobles in his own hands by this system of grants of land or money in return for military service; and the civil administration was governed on the same principle. The *mansab* and *jagir* system pervaded the whole empire. The governors of provinces were mansabdars, and received grants of land in lieu of salary for the maintenance of their state and their troops, while they were required to pay about a fifth of the revenue to the emperor. All the land in the realm was thus parcelled out among a number of *timariots*, who were practically absolute in their own districts, and extorted the uttermost farthing from the wretched peasantry who tilled their lands. The only exceptions were the royal demesnes, and these were farmed out to contractors who had all the vices without the distinction of the mansabdars. As it was always the policy of the Moghuls to shift the vassal-lords from one estate to another, in order to prevent them from acquiring a permanent local influence and prestige, the same disastrous results ensued as in the precarious appointments of Turkey. Each governor or feudatory sought to extort as much as possible out of his province, or jagir, in order to have capital in hand when he should be transplanted or deprived, and in the remoter parts of the empire the rapacity of the landholders went on almost

GOLD COIN OF AURANGZIB, STRUCK AT THATTA, A. H. 1072 (A.D. 1661-2).

unchecked. The peasantry and working classes, and even the better sort of merchants, used every precaution to hide such small prosperity as they might enjoy; they dressed and lived meanly, and suppressed all inclinations towards social ambitions.

Whether we look at the military or the civil side of the system, the Moghul domination in India was even more like an army of occupation than the "camp" to which the Ottoman Empire has been compared. As Bernier says, "The Great Moghul is a foreigner in Hindustan: he finds himself in a hostile country, or nearly so; a country containing hundreds of Gentiles to one Moghul, or even to one Mohammedan." Hence his large armies and his network of governors and landholders dependent upon him alone for dignity and support; hence, too, a policy which sacrificed the welfare of the people to the supremacy of an armed minority. Yet it preserved internal peace and secured the authority of the throne, and we read of few disturbances or insurrections in all the half-century of Aurangzib's reign. Such wars as were waged were either unimportant campaigns of aggression outside the normal limits of the empire, or were deliberately provoked by the emperor's tolerance. Mir Jumla's disastrous expedition against Assam was like many other attempts to subdue the northeast frontiers of India. The rains and the guerrilla tactics of the enemy drove the Moghul army to despair, and its gallant leader died on his return in the spring of 1663. The war in Arakan had more lasting effects. This kingdom had long been a standing menace to Bengal, and a cause of loss and dread to the traders at the mouth of the Ganges. Every kind of criminal from Goa or Ceylon, Cochin or Malacca, mostly Portuguese or half-castes, flocked to Chittagong, where the King of Arakan, delighted to welcome any sort of allies against his formidable neighbour the Moghul, permitted them to settle. They soon developed a busy trade in piracy, and, as Bernier said, "scoured the neighbouring seas in light galleys, called galleasses, entered the numerous arms and branches of the Ganges, ravaged the islands of Lower Bengal, and, often penetrating forty or fifty leagues up the country, surprised and carried away the entire population of villages. The marauders made slaves of their unhappy captives, and burnt whatever could not be removed." The Portuguese at Hugli abetted these rascals by purchasing whole cargoes of cheap slaves, and, as we have seen, were punished by Shah Jahan, who took their town and carried the remnant of the population as prisoners to Agra in 1632. But though the Portuguese power no longer availed them, the pirates continued with their rapine, and carried on operations with even greater vigour from the island of Sandip, off Chittagong, where the notorious Fra Joan, an Augustinian monk, reigned as a petty sovereign for many years, after contriving, in some mysterious way, to rid himself of the governor of the island.

When Shayista Khan, Aurangzib's uncle, came to Bengal as governor in succession to Mir Jumla, he judged it high time to put a stop to these exploits, and in 1666 the pirates submitted to the summons of the new viceroy, backed by the support of the Dutch, who were pleased to diminish the failing power of Portugal. The bulk of the freebooters were settled under control at a place a few miles below Dhakka, hence called Firengi-bazar, " the mart of the Franks," where some of their descendants still live. Shayista then sent an expedition against Arakan and annexed it, changing the name of Chittagong into Islamabad, " the city of Islam." He could not foresee that in suppressing the pirates he was aiding the rise of that future power whose humble beginnings were seen in the little factory established by the English at the Hugli in 1640. Twenty years after the suppression of the Portuguese, Charnock defeated the local militia, and in 1690 received from Aurangzib a grant of land at Sutanati, which he forthwith cleared and fortified. Such was the modest foundation of Calcutta.

CHAPTER VI

THE RUIN OF AURANGZIB

THE MARATHA WAR

1680-1707 A. D.

A PROFOUND tranquillity, broken by no rebellion of any political importance, reigned throughout Northern India for the first twenty years of Aurangzib's rule. So far there had been no serious persecution and no religious disabilities: but there can be no doubt that Aurangzib was only nursing his zeal for the faith until it should be safe to display it against the unbelievers. Indeed, there were signs of the coming storm as early as 1669. In April of that year he was informed that the Brahmans of Benares and other Hindu centres were in the habit of teaching their "wicked sciences," not only to their own people, but to Moslems. This was more than the orthodox emperor could tolerate; the temple of Vishnu at Benares was destroyed, and the splendid shrine at Mathura was razed to the ground to make room for a magnificent mosque. The idols were brought to Agra and buried under the steps of the mosque, so that good Moslems might have the satisfaction of treading them underfoot. Three years later the fanaticism of the Hindus found

MOSQUE OF AURANGZIB AT BENARES.

vent in Mewat in an obstinate insurrection of four or five thousand devotees, who called themselves Satnamis. The neighbouring Rajputs and other Hindus began to become infected with the spirit of rebellion, and every day saw fresh additions to the strength of the rioters. The Satnamis fought with the courage of despair and the exaltation of martyrs, but the end was not doubtful; thousands were slain, and the revolt was suppressed.

The next step in the policy of persecution was the reimposition of the hated jizya, or poll-tax on unbelievers, a few years later. In vain the people wailed and cursed around the palace. Aurangzib had by this time abandoned the salutary custom of appearing at stated hours before his subjects at the levee window—the adulation of the multitude savoured of idolatry to his puritanical mind. But seclude himself as he might, and thereby lose that close touch with the populace which had been his father's strength, he could not shut his eyes and ears to the uproar which the new enactment excited. When he went to the mosque, crowds of expostulating and even riotous Hindus blocked his way; and though his elephants forced their path over their bodies, he could not subdue their repugnance to the new tax on religion. His dealings with the Rajput princes kindled these sparks of discontent into a flame. He endeavoured to get Jaswant Singh's two young sons sent to Delhi to be educated (and doubtless made Moslems) under his own supervision. The Rajputs' loyalty and pride alike forbade such ignominy to their hereditary chiefs; and when they learned that the ancient law of Mohammed was revived which imposed a tax upon every soul who did not conform to Islam—a tax which Akbar had disdained, and Shah Jahan had not dared to think of—their indignation knew no bounds. They repudiated the jizya, or religious tax, and contrived to spirit away the infant princes of Marwar out of the emperor's reach.

It was the first serious rebellion during the reign,

STREET SCENE IN JODHPUR.

and its provoker little realized the effects which his fanatical policy would produce. He marched at once upon Rajputana, where he found two out of the three leading States, Udaipur (Mewar) and Jodhpur (Marwar), united against him, and only Raja Ram Singh of Jaipur (Amber) still loyal to the empire. The Rajputs kept twenty-five thousand horse, mostly Rathors of Jodhpur, in the field, and, although frequently driven into their mountains, were never really subdued. At one time they appeared to be on the point of a decisive victory, and the emperor's cause seemed lost. Directing operations from Ajmir, he had placed his main body under his fourth son, Akbar, at the same time calling up his elder sons, Mu'azzam and A'zam, with their contingents from their commands in the Deccan and Bengal. The three princes were busy ravaging the Rajput country, and Aurangzib was left at Ajmir with hardly a thousand men, when tidings came that Prince Akbar had been seduced by the diplomacy of the Rajput leaders, had gone over with the main army to the enemy, and had proclaimed himself Emperor of India; nay, more, that he was now marching against his father at the head of seventy thousand men. But the prestige, or the diplomacy, of Aurangzib was more than a match for the rebels. The Moghul deserters flocked back to the imperial standard; the Rajput army melted away; and Prince Akbar, with a following of five hundred men, fled to the Deccan, whence he eventually sailed for Persia in 1681, and never again set foot in the realm of his fathers.

The Rajput snake was scotched, but far from killed. The insults which had been offered to their chiefs and their religion, as well as the ruthless and unnecessary severity of Aurangzib's campaigns in their country, left a wound which never healed. The war went on. The Moghuls ravaged the rich lands of Udaipur, and the Rajputs retaliated by pulling down mosques and insulting the Moslems. The cities were indeed in the hands of Aurangzib, but the mountain defiles were thronged with implacable foes, who lost no opportunity of dealing a blow at the invaders. The rana of Udaipur, the chief sufferer on the Rajput side, at last succeeded in making an honourable peace with the emperor, who was tired of the struggle, and anxious to give his whole mind to the affairs of the Deccan. But while the treaty enabled Aurangzib to beat a fairly creditable retreat,

THE PALACE AT UDAIPUR.

it did not appease the indignant Rajputs of the West; even the rana of Udaipur soon rode his elephants through the treaty; and all Rajputana, except Jaipur and the eastern parts, was perpetually in a state of revolt until the end of the reign. But for his tax upon heresy, and his interference with their inborn sense of dignity and honour, Aurangzib might still have kept the Rajputs by his side as priceless allies in the long struggle in which he was now to engage in the Deccan. As it was, he alienated them for ever. So long as the great Puritan sat on the throne of Akbar, not a Rajput would stir a finger to save him. Aurangzib had to fight his southern foes with the loss of his right arm.

"Delhi is distant," says an old Deccan proverb, and many an Indian king has realized its force when grappling with the ineradicable contumacy of his southern province. The Deccan was never intended by nature to have any connection with Hindustan. The Vindhya and Satpura Mountains and the Narbada River form a triple line of natural barricades, which divide the high table-land of Central India from the plains of the Ganges and its tributaries, and should have warned the sovereigns of Delhi that it was wiser to keep to their own country. But the Deccan lands were fertile; their wealth in diamonds and gold was fabulous; and every great ruler of the northern plains has turned his eyes to the mountain barriers and longed to enter the land of promise beyond. They entered, however, at their peril. To conquer the Deccan was risking the loss of Hindustan; for he who invaded the southern people who dwelt between the Ghats was but teaching them the road to the north.

The affairs of the Deccan were no new thing to a prince who had twice been viceroy there, but some years passed before the initial difficulties of settling his kingdom left the new emperor leisure to attend to the southern province. Meanwhile a new power had arisen, a power which sprang from such needy and insignificant beginnings that no one could have foretold its future malignant domination. The Marathas began to make themselves felt.

This famous Hindu people inhabited the country lying between the Indian Ocean and the river Warda; their northern boundary was the Satpura range, and on the west coast they extended as far south as Goa. Their strength lay in the inaccessible fastnesses of the Western Ghats, which climb precipitously to the great plateau that stretches across the Deccan to the Bay of Bengal. Between the Ghats and the sea lies the Konkan, in which deep valleys and torrent-beds lead from the rocks and forests of the mountain ridge to the fertile plains of the humid tract near the sea, where the torrents merge in sandy creeks among thickets of mangroves. The Ghats and the Konkan were the safe retreats of wild beasts and wiry Marathas.

The Marathas had never made any mark in history before the reign of Shah Jahan. They were peaceful, frugal husbandmen, like the mass of the lower orders of Hindus, and gave no trouble. Their chiefs, or village headmen, were Sudras, of the lowest of the four castes, like their followers, though they pretended to connect themselves with the noble warrior caste of Kshatriyas. In the silent times of peace, the Marathas enjoyed the happiness of the nation that has no history. War brought out their dormant capacities, however, and their daggers soon cut their name deep in the annals of India. The King of Bijapur was responsible for educating this hardy race for their career of rapine. They formed a large proportion of his subjects, and their dialect, an offshoot of Sanskrit, became the official language of the revenue department of his kingdom. Gradually they came to be employed in his army, first in garrison duty, and then in the light cavalry, a branch of service for which they displayed extraordinary aptitude. Some of them rose to offices of importance at Bijapur and Golkonda. One of these officers, Shahji Bhonsla, a rebel against Shah Jahan in the Konkan in 1634, and afterwards governor of Poona and Bangalore, was the father of Sivaji, the founder of the Maratha power.

Sivaji was eight years younger than his great adversary Aurangzib. He was brought up at Poona, where he was noted for his courage and shrewdness. He mixed with the wild highlanders of the neighbouring Ghats, and, listening to their native ballads and tales of adventure, soon fell in love with their free and reckless mode of life, and learned every turn and path of the Konkan. He found that the hill forts were miserably garrisoned by the Bijapur Government, and he resolved upon seizing them and inaugurating an era of brigandage on an heroic scale. He began by surprising the castle of Torna, some twenty miles from Poona, and after adding fortress to fortress at the expense of the Bijapur kingdom without attracting much notice, crowned his iniquity in 1648 by making a convoy of royal treasure, and by occupying the whole of the northern Konkan. Presently his rule extended on the seacoast from Kaliani in the north to the neighbourhood of Portuguese Goa, a distance of over 250 miles; east of the Ghats it reached to Mirich on the Krishna; and its breadth in some parts was as much as one hundred miles. It was not a vast dominion, but it sup-

THE MIHTAR-I MAHAL AT BIJAPUR.

ported an army of over fifty thousand men, and it had been built up with incredible patience and daring.

He had no anxiety on the score of his eastern neighbour, the King of Bijapur, whose troops he routed and whose lands he plundered at will; and he now longed for fresh fields of rapine. The Hindus had become his friends, or had bought his favour, and offered few occasions for pillage. He turned, therefore, to the Moghul territory to the north, and pushed his raids almost to the gates of Aurangabad, the "Throne City." Several times Aurangzib changed his generals, but still the indomitable Marathas baffled their skill, surprised their quarters, sacked Surat—though Sir George Oxenden beat them off the English factory—and even stopped the ships full of pilgrims that were sailing from the port for Mekka. For a moment, indeed, there was peace. Serious losses induced Sivaji to make terms, and even to appear at Delhi as the emperor's vassal. The sturdy little "mountain rat," however, was out of his element at the splendid court of the Great Moghul, and Aurangzib treated him with undisguised contempt. Seldom was political sagacity more at fault. The rude highlander, who might have been converted into a powerful prop of the empire in the Deccan, was allowed to escape in disguise, affronted and enraged, to resume his old sway in the mountains in 1666. Too late the emperor attempted conciliation; the old antagonist had become a personal enemy, and nothing could soothe his resentment. His return to the Deccan was followed by a series of triumphs. Surat was again sacked in 1671, and the Maratha swarms spread southerly past Madras to Tanjore, levying blackmail wherever they went. Just as he was meditating still greater aggrandizement, a sudden illness put an end to his extraordinary career in 1680, when he was not quite fifty-three years of age. The date of his death is found in the words *Kāfir ba jahannam raft*, "The Infidel went to Hell," which is, in reality, a chronogram to be interpreted by the numerical values of the consonants (K 20, A 1, F 80, R 200, B 2, J 3, H 5, N N 50 + 50, R 200, F 80, T 400 = 1091 A. H. [1680 A. D.]).

"Sivaji always strove to maintain the honour of the people in his territories," says a Mohammedan historian. "He persisted in rebellion, plundering caravans, and troubling mankind; but he was absolutely guiltless of baser sins, and was scrupulous of the honour of women and children of the Moslems when they fell into his hands." Aurangzib himself admitted that his foe was "a great captain;" and added, "My armies have been employed against him for nineteen years, and nevertheless his state has always been increasing."

The great captain was dead, but his spirit lived in the nation he had created. Aurangzib never fully realized the strength of a nation of freebooters or the intolerable weariness of guerrilla warfare, but he at least saw that the time had come to trust no more generals, but to take the quarrel into his own hands. At the close of 1681 he arrived at Burhanpur, and took command of the army. The emperor's first step was to endeavour to strike awe into the Marathas by sending his sons to scour the country. The enemy offered no opposition, and left their rugged country to punish the invaders. Prince Mu'azzam accordingly marched through the whole Konkan, and laid it waste, and when he reached the end he found that he had hardly a horse fit to carry him, and that his men were marching afoot, half-starving. The enemy had cut down the grass, so that no fodder could be obtained, and when the Moghuls tried to victual the army by sea, the enemy intercepted the corn-ships. The rocks and forests of the Ghats had been quite as destructive to the cavalry as the spears of the Marathas. Fighting torrents and precipices, and enduring an unhealthy climate and scarcity of food was an unprofitable business; and the princes were ordered to converge upon Bijapur, while Aurangzib pushed forward to Ahmadnagar.

As soon as the enemy's back was turned, Sivaji's son, Sambhaji, swiftly led his active little horsemen behind their flank, and crossing over to Khandesh burned Burhanpur and set the whole countryside in a blaze. Before the Moghuls could get at them, they were safe again in their fastnesses in the Ghats. The stroke was typical of Maratha warfare. They never risked an engagement in the open field unless numbers made victory sure. When the heavy Moghul cavalry attacked them, these hardy little warriors, mounted on wiry steeds as inured to fatigue as themselves and splendidly broken for their tactics, would instantly scatter in all directions and observe the enemy from a neighbouring hill or wood, ready to cut off solitary horsemen, or surprise small parties in ambush; and then, if the pursuers gave up the useless chase, the Marathas were upon them in an instant, hanging on their flanks, dispatching stragglers, and firing at close quarters into the unwieldy mass. To fight such people was to do battle with the air or to strike blows upon water. The Moghul might hold as much ground as his camp and cities covered, but the rest of the Deccan was in the hands of the Marathas.

Aurangzib's plan seems to have been, first, to cut off the Marathas' funds by exterminating the kingdoms of Golkonda and Bijapur, which paid blackmail to the brigands; and then to ferret the "mountain rats" out of their holes. The first part of his programme was the less difficult. The old Deccan kingdoms were in no condition to offer serious resistance to Aurangzib's grand army. They might have been annexed long before, but for the selfish indolence of the Moghul generals. The Bijapuris indeed resorted to their usual tactics, laying waste all the country round the capital till the Moghul army was half-famished, and then hovering about its flanks and harassing its movements with a pertinacity worthy of Sivaji himself. In August, 1685, however, Aurangzib in person took command of the siege. Under his searching eye the work of intrenching and mining round the six miles of ramparts went on heartily. A close blockade was established, and at last, after more than a year's labour, Bijapur was starved out in November, 1686. The old capital of the Adil Shahs, once full of splendid palaces, became the home of the owl and jackal. It stands yet, a melancholy, silent ruin. Its beautiful mosques still raise their minarets above the stone walls, which are even now so inviolate that one might fancy he gazed upon a living city. Within, all is solitude and desolation. The "Visiapur" which astounded so many travellers by its wealth and magnificence, was trampled under the foot of the puritan emperor, and fell to rise no more.

Golkonda soon felt the loss of its protecting sister. It had always pushed forward its neighbour as a buffer to deaden the shock of the Moghul assaults. It had

THE GREAT MOSQUE OF BIJAPUR.

secretly subsidized Bijapur to enable it to defend itself against the Moghuls, and at the same time bribed the imperial officers to attack Bijapur rather than itself. In spite of its ingenuity, Golkonda had been forced to bow the knee before Aurangzib in 1656, and had been growing more and more demoralized in the quarter of a century which had rolled by uneasily since that year.

Prince Mu'azzam besieged the capital in a half-hearted way in 1685, and then, to his father's disgust, consented to a treaty of peace. Nevertheless, Aurangzib resolved to make an end of the Kutb Shah dynasty. Under cover of a pilgrimage to a holy shrine, he marched to Kulbarga, half-way to Golkonda. His hostile intentions were unmistakable. The wretched king, Abu-l-Hasan, knew that his fall was at hand. In vain he sent submissive messages to the emperor and laid his humble protestations of obedience at his feet; Aurangzib was relentless, and seeing that there was no hope of mercy the King of Golkonda prepared to die like a soldier. He cast off his sloth and luxury of life, and set about ordering his army and making ready for the siege of his citadel.

In January, 1687, the enemy took ground at gunshot range, and the leaguer began. Abu-l-Hasan had forty or fifty thousand horse outside the walls which continually harassed the engineers, and the garrison plied their cannon and rockets with deadly effect upon the trenches. The defence was heroic; frequent and furious were the sallies; the fortress was well found in ammunition and provisions, and a ceaseless fire was kept up night and day from the gates and ramparts. At last the lines were pushed up to the fosse, and Aurangzib himself sewed the first sack that was to be filled with earth and thrown into the ditch. Heavy guns were mounted on earthworks to keep back the defenders, and an attempt was made to scale the walls by night. Some of the besiegers had already gained the ramparts, when a dog gave the alarm, and the garrison speedily dispatched the climbers and threw down the ladders.

Meanwhile famine was reducing the Moghul army to extremities. The friends of Golkonda, and especially the Marathas of "that hell-dog" Sambhaji, laid the country waste; the season was dry, and there was a terrible scarcity of rice, grain, and fodder. Plague broke out in the camp, and many of the soldiers, worn out with hunger and misery, deserted to the enemy. When the rain came at last, it fell in torrents for three days, and washed away much of the entrenchments, whereupon the besieged sallied out in force and killed many of the Moghuls, and took prisoners. The occasion seemed favourable for overtures of peace. Abu-l-Hasan showed his prisoners the heaps of corn and treasure in the fort, and offered to pay an indemnity and to supply the besieging army with grain, if the siege were raised. Aurangzib's answer was full of his old proud inflexible resolve: "Abu-l-Hasan must come to me with clasped hands, or he shall come bound; I will then consider what mercy I can show him." Forthwith he ordered fifty thousand fresh sacks from Berar to fill the moat.

Where courage and perseverance failed, treason succeeded. Mines and assaults had been vainly tried against the heroic defenders of Golkonda; money and promises at last won the day. Many of the nobles of the city had from time to time gone over to the besiegers, and at length a bribe admitted the enemy. The

Moghuls poured into the fortress and raised a shout of triumph. The only faithful amir, Abd-ar-Razzak, heard it, and leaping on a bare-backed horse, followed by a dozen retainers, galloped to the gate, through which the enemy were rushing. Covered with blood and reeling in his saddle, he found his way out, and they found him next day lying senseless under a cocoanut tree, with more than seventy wounds.

He was the hero of the siege. Aurangzib said that had Abu-l-Hasan possessed but one more servant as loyal as this, the contest might have gone on much longer. He sent a European and a Hindu surgeon to attend to the wounded man, and rejoiced when after sixteen days he at last opened his eyes. He showered favours upon the hero's sons, but nothing could shake the loyalty of the father. Lying on his sick-bed, he said that "no man who had eaten salt of Abu-l-Hasan could enter the service of Aurangzib." Contrasted with the universal self-seeking of the Moghul Court, such faithfulness was rare indeed, and no one honoured it more sincerely than the emperor who had never been disloyal to his standard of duty.

Meanwhile Abu-l-Hasan had heard the shouts and groans, and knew that his hour was come. He went into the harem and tried to comfort the women, and then, asking their pardon for his faults, he bade them farewell, and taking his seat in the audience-chamber waited calmly for his unbidden guests. He would not suffer his dinner-hour to be postponed for such a trifle as the Moghul conquest. When the officers of Aurangzib appeared, he saluted them as became a king, and spoke to them in choice Persian. He then called for his horse and rode with them to Prince A'zam, who presented him to Aurangzib. The Great Moghul treated him with grave courtesy, as king to king, for the gallantry of his defence of Golkonda atoned for his many sins of the past. He was then sent a prisoner to Dau-

FORT OF GOLKONDA.

latabad, where his ally of Bijapur was already a captive, and both their dynasties disappear from history, while Aurangzib appropriated a sum equivalent to about seven millions sterling from the royal property of Golkonda.

With the conquest of Golkonda and Bijapur, Aurangzib considered himself master of the Deccan. Yet the direct result of this destruction of the only powers that made for order and some sort of settled government in the peninsula was to strengthen the hands of the Marathas. The majority of the vanquished armies naturally joined them, and adopted the calling of the road. The local officials set themselves up as petty sovereigns, and gave the brigands support, as the party most likely to promote a golden age of plunder. Thus the bulk of the population of the two dissolved states went to swell the power of Sambhaji and his highlanders, and the disastrous results of this revolution in Deccan politics were felt for more than a century.

At first, indeed, Aurangzib's armies seemed to carry all before them, and the work of taking possession of the whole territory of the vanished kingdoms, even as far south as Mysore, was swiftly accomplished. Sivaji's brother was hemmed in at Tanjore, and the Marathas were everywhere driven away to their mountain forts. To crown these successes, Sambhaji was captured by some enterprising Moghuls at a moment of careless self-indulgence. Brought before Aurangzib, he displayed his talents for vituperation and blasphemy to such a degree that he was put to death with circumstances of exceptional barbarity in 1689. The brigands were awed for a while by the commanding personality and irresistible force of the Great Moghul. He had accomplished a military occupation, not merely of the Deccan, but of the whole peninsula, save the extreme point south of Trichinopoly and the marginal possessions of the Portuguese and other foreigners. Military occupation, however, was not enough, and he determined to make the southern provinces an integral part of his settled empire, as finally and organically a member of it as the

Marble Fretwork Screen around the Tomb in the Taj Mahal.
From a Photograph.

Panjab or Bengal. With this aim he stayed on and on, till hope and will, unquenchable in life, were stilled in death. The exasperating struggle lasted seventeen years after the execution of Sambhaji and the capture of his chief stronghold, and at the end success was as far off as ever.

The explanation of this colossal failure is to be found partly in the contrast between the characters of the invaders and the defenders. Had the Moghuls been the same hardy warriors that Babar led from the valleys of the Hindu Kush, or had the Rajputs been the loyal heroes who had so often courted destruction in their devoted service of earlier emperors, the Marathas would have been allowed but a short shrift. But Aurangzib had alienated the Rajputs for ever, and they would not risk their lives for him in exterminating a people who were, after all, Hindus, however inferior to themselves in caste and dignity. As for the Moghuls, three or four generations of court-life had ruined their ancient manliness. Babar would have scorned to command such officers as surrounded Aurangzib in his gigantic camp at Bairampur. Instead of hardy swordsmen, they had become padded dandies. They were adorned for a procession, when they should have been in rough campaigning outfit. Their camp was as splendid and luxurious as if they were on guard at the Palace of Delhi. The very rank and file grumbled if their tents were not furnished as comfortably as in quarters at Agra, and their requirements attracted an immense crowd of camp-followers, twenty times as numerous as the effective strength. So vast a host was like a plague of locusts in the country; it devoured everything, and though at times it was richly provisioned, at others the Marathas cut off communications with the base of supplies in the north, and a famine speedily ensued.

The Marathas, on the other hand, cared nothing for luxuries: a cake of millet sufficed them for a meal, with perhaps an onion for relish. They defended a fort to the last, and then defended another fort. They were pursued from place to place, but were never daunted, and they filled up the intervals of sieges by harassing the Moghul armies, stopping convoys of supplies, and laying the country waste in the path of the enemy. There was no bringing them to a decisive engagement. It was one long series of petty victories followed by larger losses. Nothing was gained that was worth the labour; more and more the Marathas became objects of dread to the demoralized Moghul army; and the country, exasperated at the sufferings of a prolonged occupation by an alien and licentious soldiery, became increasingly devoted to the cause of the intrepid bandits, which they identified as their own.

The marvellous thing about this wearisome campaign of twenty years is the way in which the brave old emperor endured its many hardships and disappointments. It was he who planned every campaign, issued all the general orders, selected the points for attack and the lines of entrenchment, and controlled every movement of his various divisions in the Deccan. He conducted many of the sieges in person, and when a mine exploded among the besiegers at Sattara in 1699, and general despondency fell on the army, the octogenarian mounted his horse and rode to the scene of disaster "as if in search of death." He piled the bodies of the dead into a human ravelin, and was with difficulty prevented from leading the assault himself. He was still the man who had chained his elephant at the battle of Samugarh forty years before. Nor was his energy confined to the overwhelming anxieties of the war. His orders extended to affairs in Afghanistan and disturbances at Agra; he even thought of retaking Kandahar. Not an officer, not a government clerk, was appointed without his knowledge, and the conduct of the whole official staff was vigilantly scrutinized with the aid of an army of spies.

We are fortunate in possessing a portrait of Aurangzib, as he appeared in the midst of his Deccan campaigns. On Monday, the 21st of March, 1695, Dr. Gemelli Careri was admitted to an audience with the emperor in his quarters, called "Gulalbar," at the camp of Galgala. He saw an old man with a white beard, trimmed round, contrasting vividly with his olive skin; "he was of low stature, with a large nose; slender and stooping with age." Sitting upon rich carpets, and leaning against gold-embroidered cushions, he received the Neapolitan courteously, asked his business in the camp, and being told of Careri's travels in Turkey, made inquiries about the war then raging between the Sultan and the princes of Hungary. The doctor saw him again at the public audience in a great tent pitched within a court enclosed by screens of painted calico. The Moghul appeared leaning on a crutched staff and preceded by several nobles. He was simply dressed in a white robe tied under the right arm with a silk sash from which his dagger hung. On his head was a white turban bound with a gold web, "on which an emeraud of a vast bigness appear'd amidst four little ones. His shoes were after the Moorish fashion, and his legs naked without hose." He took his seat upon a square gilt throne raised two steps above the daïs, which was inclosed with silver banisters; three brocaded pillows formed the sides and back, and in front was a little silver footstool. Over his head a servant held a green umbrella to keep off the sun, while two others whisked the flies away with long white horsetails. "When he was seated they gave him his scimitar and buckler, which he laid down on his left side within the throne. Then he made a sign with his hand for those that had business to draw near; who being come up, two secretaries, standing, took their petitions, which they delivered to the king, telling him the contents. I admir'd to see him indorse them with his own hand, without spectacles, and by his cheerful smiling countenance seemed to be pleased with the employment."

AN INDIAN DAGGER.

It is a striking picture of the vigorous old age of one who allowed no faculty of his active mind to rust, no spring of his spare frame to relax. But behind that serene mask lay a gloomy, lonely soul. It was the pathetic fate of the Moghul emperor to live and die alone. Solitary state was the heritage of his rank, and his natural bent of mind widened the breach that severed him from those around him. The fate of Shah Jahan preyed upon his mind. He was wont to remind his sons that he was not one to be treated as he had used his own father. His eldest son had paid the penalty of his brief and flighty treason by a lifelong captivity; and Aurangzib had early impressed the lesson upon the second brother. "The art of reigning," he told Mu'azzam, "is so delicate, that a king must be jealous of his own shadow. Be wise, or a fate like your brother's will befall you also." Mu'azzam had been docility personified, but his father's restless suspicion was aroused more than once, and from 1687 to 1694 he endured a rigorous captivity. On his release, another brother, A'zam, became in turn the object of jealousy, and it is said that he never received a letter from his father without turning pale. One son after another was tried and found wanting. Towards the close of his life the jealous father was drawn closer to his youngest son, Kam Bakhsh, whose mother, Udaipuri Bai, was the only woman for whom the emperor entertained anything approaching real love. The young prince was suspected of trafficking the imperial honour with the Marathas and was placed under temporary arrest, but his father forgave or acquitted him, and his last letters breathe a tone of tender affection.

The end of the lonely unloved life was approaching.

Failure stamped every effort of the final years. The emperor's long absence had given the rein to disorders in the north; the Rajputs were in open rebellion, the Jats had risen about Agra, and the Sikhs began to make their name notorious in Multan. The Deccan was a desert, where the path of the Marathas was traced by pillaged towns, ravaged fields, and smoking villages. The Moghul army was enfeebled and demoralized; "those infernal foot-soldiers" were croaking like rooks in an invaded rookery, clamouring for their arrears of pay. The finances were in hopeless confusion, and Aurangzib refused to be troubled with them. The Marathas became so bold that they plundered on the skirts of the Grand Army and openly scoffed at the emperor, and no man dared leave the Moghul lines without a strong escort. There was even a talk of making terms with the insolent bandits.

At last the emperor led the dejected remnant of his once powerful army, in confusion and alarm, and pursued by skirmishing bodies of exultant Marathas, back to Ahmadnagar, whence, more than twenty years before, he had set out, full of sanguine hope and at the head of a splendid and invincible host. His long privations had at length told upon his health, and when he entered the city he said that his journeys were over. Even when convinced that the end was near, his invincible suspicions still mastered his natural affections. He kept all his sons away, lest they should do even as he had done to his own father. Alone he had lived, and alone he made ready to die. He had all the puritan's sense of sin and unworthiness, and his morbid creed inspired a terrible dread of death. He poured out his troubled heart to his sons in letters which show the love which all his suspicion could not uproot.

"Peace be with you and yours," he wrote to Prince A'zam, "I am grown very old and weak, and my limbs are feeble. Many were around me when I was born, but now I am going alone. I know not why I am or wherefore I came into the world. I bewail the moments which I have spent forgetful of God's worship. I have not done well by the country or its people. My years have gone by profitless. God has been in my heart, yet my darkened eyes have not recognized his light. Life is transient, and a moment lost never returns. There is no hope for me in the future. The fever is gone: but only skin and dried flesh are mine. The army is confounded and without heart or help, even as I am, apart from God, with no rest for the heart. They know not whether they have a king or not. I brought nothing into this world, but I carry away with me the burthen of my sins. I know not what punishment be in store for me to suffer. Though my trust is in the mercy and goodness of God, I deplore my sins. When I have lost hope in myself, how can I hope in others? Come what will, I have launched my bark upon the waters. Farewell! Farewell! Farewell!"

To his favourite son, Kam Bakhsh, he wrote: "Soul of my soul. Now I am going alone. I grieve for your helplessness. But what is the use? Every torment I have inflicted, every sin I have committed, every wrong

I have done, I carry the consequence with me. Strange that I came with nothing into the world, and now go away with this stupendous caravan of sin! Wherever I look I see only God. I have greatly sinned, and I know not what torment awaits me. Let not Moslems be slain and reproach fall upon my useless head. I commit you and your sons to God's care, and bid you farewell. I am sorely troubled. Your sick mother Udaipuri would fain die with me. Peace!"

On Friday, the 4th of March, 1707, in the fiftieth year of his reign, and the eighty-ninth of his life, after performing the morning prayers and repeating the creed, the emperor Aurangzib gave up the ghost. In accordance with his command, "Carry this creature of dust to the nearest burial-place, and lay him in the earth with no useless coffin," he was buried in all simplicity near Daulatabad beside the tombs of Moslem saints.

"Every plan that he formed came to little good; every enterprise failed": such is the comment of the Mohammedan historian on the career of the sovereign whom he justly extols for his "devotion, austerity, and justice," and his "incomparable courage, long-suffering, and judgment." Aurangzib's life had been a vast failure, indeed, but he had failed grandly. It is his glory that he could not force his soul, that he dared not desert the colours of his faith. The great Puritan of India was of such stuff as wins the martyr's crown.

CHAPTER VII

THE FALL OF THE MOGHUL EMPIRE

THE HINDU REVIVAL

1707-1765 A. D.

AURANGZIB was the last of the Great Moghuls, in all save the name. He had been by far the most powerful of the line; he had ruled wider territories and commanded vaster armies than Akbar; and he had governed his teeming populations with an absolute despotism in which no other man had a voice. What Akbar had achieved by broad-minded statesmanship, and Shah Jahan by imposing majesty and panoplied array, Aurangzib had accomplished by the exercise of an iron will and indomitable personal labour. Through the greater part of his long reign no sovereign was ever more abjectly feared and obeyed; certainly none showed a more marvellous grasp of administration. Then, at the last, the effects of too close repression, of overgovernment, and of excessive centralization were discovered. The tedious war in the Deccan exhausted his armies and destroyed his prestige, and no sooner was the dominating mind stilled in death than all the forces that he had sternly controlled, all the warring elements that had struggled for emancipation from the grinding yoke, broke out in irrepressible tumult. Even before the end of his reign Hindustan was in confusion, and the signs of coming dissolution had appeared. As some imperial corpse, preserved for ages in its dread seclusion, crowned and armed and still majestic, falls to dust at the mere breath of heaven, so fell the empire of the Moghul when the great name that guarded it was no more. To adapt an image drawn by Keene from the well-known Indian tree *ficus religiosa*, it was as though some splendid palace, reared with infinite skill with all the costliest stones and precious metals of the earth, had attained its perfect beauty only to collapse in undistinguishable ruin when the insidious roots of the creeper sapped the foundations.

Even had Aurangzib left a successor of his own mental and moral stature, it may be doubted whether the process of disintegration could have been stayed. The disease was too far advanced for even the most heroic surgery. To increase the confusion, the Great Moghul had made no nomination to the throne he was vacating, and as usual all the sons claimed the sceptre. The contest was brief; Prince A'zam was slain in battle near Agra, Kam Bakhsh died of his wounds after a defeat near Haidarabad, and the first-born, Mu'azzam, ascended the throne with the title of Bahadur Shah. He found himself face to face with such difficulties as had not been known since the days of Humayun. It was not merely the Marathas that had to be dealt with; the Rajput rajas were in revolt; the Sikhs were rising in the Panjab, and the Jats near Agra; and the English had ventured on bold reprisals, which were to lead to far-reaching consequences in another half-century.

A SIKH QUOIT-TURBAN.
With knives and tiger claws, the special Sikh weapons.

Nor was it only among non-Moslem peoples that the spirit of insurrection was alive. These, no doubt, had been excited by the religious intolerance of the late emperor; but the Moslems themselves were scarcely in better order. The fatal system of rewarding services or conciliating jealousies by large grants of territory had produced a kind of baronage fully as dangerous and subversive of central authority as any corresponding class in feudal Europe. The provincial mansabdars had become petty kings, and were far more interested in coercing their neighbours than in supporting their emperor against his many foes. Nor could Bahadur rely upon his troops as Babar and Akbar had trusted them. The toleration of Akbar's policy and the luxurious splendour of Shah Jahan's court had bred both indifference and effeminacy in what had once been an army of hardy mountaineers. India had proved the Capua of Babar's veterans, and the enervating climate had relaxed their thews and softened their training, while drink had become the curse not only of the imperial house, many of whom died of it, but also of the nobles and the whole court. As Sir William Hunter has said, "The heroic soldiers of the early empire and their not less heroic wives had given place to a vicious and delicate breed of grandees. The ancestors of Aurangzib, who swooped down on India from the north, were ruddy men in boots: the courtiers among whom Aurangzib grew up were pale persons in petticoats. Babar, the founder of the empire, had swum every river which he met with during thirty years of campaigning; the luxurious nobles around the youthful Aurangzib wore skirts made of innumerable folds of the finest white muslin, and went to war in palankins." Nothing but the old emperor's steel hand and high example could have made these men join in his campaigns; but even so, twenty years of doubtful warfare had exhausted what courage there was, and his successor inherited a thoroughly dispirited army.

With such materials as he had, and against such odds, Bahadur must be credited with both courage and prudence. He showed no rancour against the chiefs who had sided with his brothers in the brief war of succession, but gladly welcomed them to his councils. His great object was to settle affairs in the Deccan so as to be free to deal with the many troubles in Hindustan. Fortunately, there was a split among the Marathas, and two claimants to the chief command, one of whom, the rightful heir, was a captive in the Moghul camp. This Sahu was released by Bahadur, who recognized his title on conditions of peace. Leaving the Marathas to arrange their own differences, the emperor went north and made terms with the insurgent Rajputs, practically restoring them to the position they had held in Akbar's reign. The terms might have been less favourable if Bahadur's anxieties had not been concentrated on a new danger.

The Sikhs, who had begun about two centuries before as a purely religious sect of theists, had been driven by Moslem persecution to form themselves into a military organization, with distinctive uniform, customs, and ceremonies; and by the close of the seventeenth century they had developed into a fierce and fanatical soldiery, burning to avenge the atrocities suffered by their leader, Guru Govind, at the hands of the Moslems. The general confusion at the time of Aurangzib's death gave them their opportunity. From their retreats on the upper Sutlaj they raided the eastern Panjab, butchering their enemies, men, women, and children, and destroying the mosques. A second raid, as far as Lahore and even Delhi, brought Bahadur into the field. He drove them to the hills, but without materially shaking their power; and then, unfortunately, he died in 1712. Short as his reign had been, it must be remembered that he was the son of a very old man, and was himself nearly seventy. Had he been in the prime of life, there might possibly have been a different story to tell.

After the usual struggle for the throne and ensuing massacre of kindred, he was succeeded by his son, Jahandar, utterly incapable and incurably vicious; in less than a year he was murdered, and his nephew, Farrukhsiyar, a despicable poltroon, suffered the like fate six years later (1719). Then, after a couple of youths had been tried for a few months, Mohammad Shah received the title of emperor, which he retained for twenty-eight years. It was but a title, however, for the power and the glory had departed from the house of Babar, and Mohammad was able only to preserve some semblance of authority by intrigue and combination with the various governors and adventurers who now partitioned the distracted empire. By such means he contrived to rid himself of the dictatorship of the Barha Sayyids, two brothers who for some years had usurped the supreme control of affairs in the time of their wretched tool, Farrukhsiyar. But there were other forces which he could not master.

Among these the Sikhs were no longer to be reckoned, for they had been put down in the time of the Sayyids with remorseless brutality, and for many years this valiant people was scarcely heard of. The Marathas, on the other hand, were increasing in power every year. Their only rival in the Deccan was Chin Kulich Khan, better known as Asaf Jah, the founder of the dynasty of the Nizams of Haidarabad which exists to this day; and Asaf Jah found it expedient to make terms with the enemy and to submit to their system of levying the *chauth*, a kind of Danegeld by means of which the Marathas systematically extended their influence with less trouble than if they had immediately insisted on territorial cessions. By the skilful policy of Balaji, and his even abler son, Baji Rao, the earliest of the Peshwas — the real leaders, who stood towards the hereditary Maratha raja much as the Shogan did to the Mikado before the Japanese revolution — this system of blackmail was enlarged until it was accepted not only in the Deccan, but in Gujarat, Malwa, and even as far north as Bandelkhand. By this time some famous names, such as Pilaji Gaikwar, Holkar, and Sindhai began to appear among the officers of the peshwa, and save for old Asaf Jah, who was now the leading man in India, there was no corresponding ability on the Moghul side. Even this veteran, when the Marathas, by way of demonstration, advanced to the very gates of Delhi, could muster only thirty-four thousand men to oppose them. The result was the cession of the whole of the territories between the Narbada and the Chambal to the successful peshwa in 1738.

While the wolves of the Deccan were steadily working up from the south, a new catastrophe from the north befell the vestiges of the Moghul empire. In the midst of the pressing difficulties that surrounded them, neither the emperors nor their ministers had been able to pay much attention to what was going on in Afghanistan. Kabul and Ghazni still belonged to the empire of Delhi, as they had done since the time of Babar, but Kandahar, which had been in the possession of the Shahs of Persia since 1648, had been seized by the Ghilzai Afghans, who had carried their successes to the point of seating their chief upon the Persian throne in 1722. Their brief triumph was reversed seven years later, by the famous soldier Nadir Shah, who not only gained possession of Persia, but recovered Kandahar in 1738, and immediately completed his conquest by seizing Kabul and Ghazni. The Moghuls, by what should form an instructive precedent, relied on the mountain tribes, whom they had formerly subsidized, to prevent the invaders from penetrating the passes into India; but the subsidy had lapsed during the recent troubles, and the Afghans offered no obstacles to the Persians. In November, 1738, Nadir crossed the Indus, and after a partial engagement with the Moghul forces, who were half disposed to side with the invaders, the conqueror received the surrender of the emperor in February, 1739. The Persians entered Delhi with Mohammad Shah as their captive guest, and in revenge for a murderous onslaught of the populace, the capital was given over to fire, carnage, and rapine. The imperial treasures, including the famous jewelled Peacock Throne, valued by Tavernier at £6,000,000, were seized and transported to Persia, the inhabitants were squeezed to the last penny, and torture was employed to extort payment. "Sleep and rest forsook the city. In every chamber and house was heard the cry of affliction. It was before a general massacre, but now the murder of individuals." The awful visitation of Timur was repeated and even outdone. At last, after two months of colossal pillage, Nadir re-

THE PEACOCK THRONE, NOW IN TEHERAN.

turned to his own country, carrying with him spoils equivalent to eight or nine millions in money alone, besides an immense treasure of gold and silver plate, jewels, rich stuffs, and a crowd of skilled artisans, with herds of elephants, horses, and camels.

This invasion of India from the north, unexpected as it was after a cessation of all such inroads during two centuries of Moghul power, was too successful not to invite repetition, and upon the assassination of Nadir in 1747, Ahmad Shah, the chief of the Abdali tribe of Afghans, after founding a powerful kingdom at Kandahar, soon found his way into the Panjab. This first attempt was strenuously resisted in 1748, and the battle of Sirhind saw the Afghans driven back by Indian troops as they were never repulsed again; but Ahmad Shah did not abandon his design. The empire of Delhi was at its weakest; the old nizam was dead, and the factions at court were internecine. The new emperor, also named Ahmad, who succeeded Mohammad in 1748, was so sorely beset by the Rohillas that he, or rather his vizir Safdar Jang, nawab or viceroy of Oudh, the first to combine the offices of nawab and vizir, was reduced to the necessity of calling the Marathas to his aid. Holkar and Sindhia enabled the vizir to bring the Rohillas to submission, but the Deccan wolves indemnified themselves liberally for their help, by levying *chauth* throughout the conquered districts. Even Bengal had been forced to submit to their blackmail, and the Marathas were now in a position to dictate terms at Delhi. Indeed, the empire of Aurangzib had lost the power of resistance. Not a province of all the wide dominion that still nominally owned the Moghul's sway was really under his control, except the upper Doab and a few districts about the Sutlaj. The Panjab was in the hands of the Afghans, Safdar Jang was practically sovereign at Oudh and Allahabad, and Ali Verdi Khan held Bengal. Afghans and Rohillas did as they pleased in the middle Doab and Rohilkhand, Gujarat and Malwa were Maratha provinces, and the Deccan, even the part held by the second nizam, was wholly beyond the mastery of Delhi.

Meanwhile, Ahmad Shah still hovered over the Panjab, which was tamely ceded to him in the hope of checking worse demands; but a treacherous attack on his governor at Lahore roused him to a fresh invasion, and in 1756 Delhi again experienced all the horrors of a sack. When he withdrew in the following year, the old intrigues and jealousies revived; the Marathas were again called in, and this time the peshwa's brother actually occupied the capital, where a new puppet-emperor, Alamgir II, who had succeeded the debauched Ahmad in 1754, was helpless between the rival interests of the vizir, Ghazi-ad-din, and the Afghan chief of Rohilla, Najib-ad-daulah. The Marathas now made themselves masters of the Panjab, and felt that they were within sight of the conquest of the whole of Hindustan. They were in the zenith of their power. Their domestic differences had been accommodated, and a general combination of all their forces was arranged. They were no longer the ill-disciplined band of marauders that had baffled Aurangzib by their guerrilla tactics; besides such predatory hordes, they had well-ordered cavalry and infantry, and a better artillery train than the Moghuls themselves. Full of their strength and ambition, they raised the cry of Hindustan for the Hindus.

It had become a religious war, centred round the

phantom of the Moghul empire. On the one hand was the Mohammedan Afghan, Ahmad Shah, eager to recover the Panjab and to take vengeance on the new power that had robbed him. On the other was the Moghul vizir of Oudh, Shuja‘-ad-daulah, son of Safdar Jang, supported by the forces of the eastern provinces. Between lay the prostrate capital, overawed by the host of the Hindu Marathas. There was not even a Moghul emperor to hold the balance, for the harmless figurehead, Alamgir, had been murdered by the vizir in 1759, and the heir, Shah Alam, had fled to the protection of the British in Bengal in dread of sharing the same fate. Among all the bold adventurers who played the king in India at this time, none was more remarkable than Ghazi-ad-din, the youthful grand-nephew of Asaf Jah, who dominated the political situation from 1752 to 1759 by sheer audacity and brilliant recklessness. The murder of the emperor, however, was a stroke that overreached itself, and when the Afghan Shah moved down upon the capital, the unscrupulous young assassin fled for his life. Ahmad Shah found the throne empty, and proceeded, as master of the situation, to take steps for the maintenance of the Mohammedan power in India.

The decisive moment came on January 6, 1761. The Marathas were intrenched at Panipat with a force of 70,000 cavalry and 15,000 infantry, nine thousand of whom were thoroughly disciplined under a Mohammedan who had served in the French army in India under Bussy. The commander-in-chief was the pesh-

EASTERN AFGHAN TYPES.
(From Roskoschny's Afghanistan.)

wa's cousin, Sadasheo Bhao, and Holkar and Sindhia were with him. The Afghans and Moghuls numbered about 53,000 horse, Afghan, Persian, and Indian, and less than 40,000 infantry, partly Rohillas under Najib; but their field-pieces were very inferior to the Marathas' guns. Too weak to attack, the Moslem army intrenched itself over against the Hindus, and for two months the opposing forces that were contending for the crown of India watched each other narrowly. Famine soon began to make itself felt, but Ahmad Shah refused to force an action. He knew that the Deccan wolves were suffering even more than his Patans and were even opening negotiations for peace with the nawab-vizir, although the Afghan king, strongly urged by Najib, refused all compromise.

At last the Bhao declared that the cup was full to the brim and could not hold another drop; the time for negotiation was past, and the starved Hindus, smeared with turmeric, rushed upon the Afghan army. For a time it looked as if Hinduism had triumphed. The Rohillas suffered tremendously; the vizir could hardly hold his ground; the Moslems were skulking or flying. Ahmad Shah, who was watching the battle from his red tent, saw that the time had come to order up his reserves. He rallied the fugitives, cut down all who would not return to the fight, and sent his mailed reserve, 10,000 strong, to support the vizir and charge upon the enemy in close order. The effect of this heavy charge at the close of an exhausting battle was supreme. The Marathas gave way, the Bhao was killed, Holkar and Sindhia left the field, and an awful butchery followed. Once more the plain of Panipat had witnessed a decisive battle in the history of India.

The Marathas never recovered from the blow, though they had still a prominent part to play in the annals of Hindustan. For the present the scene of action was transferred from Delhi to Bengal and Bihar, where the new emperor, Shah Alam, was involved in the complicated difficulties that had sprung up between the nawab-vizir and the British. Here, however, the history of Mohammedan India closes, and the history of British India begins. The victory of Panipat swept the Marathas away only to make a clear path for the English. Less than four years afterwards the battle of Baxar (Baksar), on October 23, 1764, disposed of the power of the nawab, and the next day Shah Alam came into the British camp. The treaty then signed made the nawab-vizir a vassal of Calcutta and the Moghul emperor a pensioner of the East India Company. Such was the political tragedy of the famous House of Timur.

The dynasty of Babar ended in nothingness, like all its many predecessors. The Mohammedan ascendency in Hindustan, rising from Mahmud's raids, spreading under the vigorous rule of a few of the Slave Kings and their great successor, Ala-ad-din, and attaining its widest scope and severest aspect under Aurangzib, only to fall rapidly to its decline in the weak hands of his descendants, left few traces of its long domination. A new vernacular, compounded of the languages of the Shah Namah and the Ramayana; a multitude of exquisite monuments of the Moslem faith, inspired by analogies in far western lands of Islam, but modified, and, if one may say so, sensualized by the grosser architecture of India; a few provinces still owning Mohammedan rulers; a large Moslem minority content to dwell among "infidels" and to obey the behests of the Christians from the distant islands of the West — such are the chief legacies of Islam to India. Nine centuries of association have produced no sensible fusion between the Moslem and the Hindu, any more than two centuries of intercourse have blended either with the dominant English. There are those who believe that the contact of Western energy with Eastern thought, the infusion of European literature in the subtle Indian mind, and the reaction of the ancient philosophies of the Brahman schools upon the imagination of the West, may end in generating a new force in the world, perchance an Indian nation combining the profound speculations of the East with the progressive activities of Europe. Prophecy is no part of the historian's duty; but if any forecast may be deduced from the long period of alien rule surveyed in the preceding pages, it is not favourable to any hopes of such a consummation. The conquerors of India have come in hordes again and again, but they have scarcely touched the soul of the people. The Indian is still, in the main, what he always was, in spite of them all; and however forcible the new and unprecedented influences now at work upon an instructed minority, one can with difficulty imagine any serious change in the rooted character and time-honoured instincts of the vast mass of the people, nor is it at all certain that such change would be for the better.

APPENDIXES

APPENDIX I

AKBAR'S CAPTURE OF FORT ASIR

FROM THE AKBAR-NAMAH OF ILLAHBAD FAIZI OF SIRHIND

(*An Extract translated from the Persian by Dowson in Elliot's History of India*)

The extract here presented is from an abridged account of certain important events in the reign of Akbar the Great compiled by Shaikh Illahbad Faizi of Sirhind from the fuller and more important *Tabakāt-i Akbarī* of Nizam-ad-din and the well-known *Akbar Nāmah* of Abu-l-Fazl. The chronicler, after giving an account of the rebellions raised against the rule of Akbar by the Mirzas of Surat in 1572 (see p. 13), draws a graphic picture of the great emperor's campaigns in the Deccan, and especially of the storming, in 1600, of the fortress of Asir, the most impregnable fortress in Khandesh, a district now comprised in the Bombay Presidency (see p. 49).

EDITOR.

THE Emperor Akbar had subjected to his rule the whole wide expanse of Hindustan, with the exception of a portion of the Deccan, the rulers of which had, nevertheless, in former years sent representatives and presents to the Imperial throne. Some of these rulers, however, had since failed in duly discharging their obligations and had thus wounded the pride of the emperor. Prince Shah Murad, Khan-khanan, and other amirs had been sent to effect the conquest of the country. The prince went to that country and distinguished himself by his services. Other amirs were afterwards sent, who fought bravely, and subjugated a considerable portion of the district. The work of conquest was still progressing, when it entered the heart of Prince Salim, who later became Shah Jahangir, that he would proceed thither to support the amirs and to accomplish the reduction of the remainder of the country, so that diversities of religion might be swept away and that the whole country might repose in peace under the Imperial rule. For five or six years the conquest had been retarded by the bickerings of the amirs, and he consequently resolved to proceed from Lahore to the Imperial presence at Agra, there to obtain information of the true state of affairs, because that place was nearer to the scene of action, and after due consultation to proceed thither in person, should it seem necessary.

THE OLD OBSERVATORY AT UJJAIN.

When intelligence arrived of the death of Prince Shah Murad, Prince Daniyal was sent to the Deccan; but Akbar, not feeling at ease regarding the state of affairs in that province, resolved to proceed toward it by making a hunting excursion to Malwa. His intention was to send a strong reinforcement to Prince Daniyal under Bahadur, son of Raja Ali of Khandesh, and to rest a while in Malwa till events took a favourable turn. The emperor accordingly left Agra, and on the 21st of the month, after showing great honour and favour to Khan-khanan, he sent him on in advance. On the 7th of Rabi-as-sani, the emperor reached Dholpur. The river Chambal was crossed by fords and his Majesty went over on an elephant. On the 17th he reached the fort of Gwalior. On the 29th of Jumad-as-sani, he passed through Sironj, and on the 1st of Rajab the royal camp was pitched between Kaliyada and Ujjain. This city Ujjain is one of the most ancient in Hindustan and contains many relics of antiquity. Kaliyada is the name of one of the most delightful places in the world. Here the emperor rested for a while, expecting that Bahadur Khan, son of Raja Ali Khan of Khandesh, would come to wait upon him.

Raja Ali of Khandesh had been slain fighting bravely under Khan-khanan against the Deccan troops, and it was expected that his son would now come forward to give his services to the Imperial army in the hope of revenging his father's fall and of gaining the Imperial favour. Even while the emperor was encamped at Ujjain, some intimation was received about his intentions, and he now sent an envoy to the emperor, charged with many excuses and foolish evasions. Hereupon his Majesty, in his great kindness, sent the chief-justice Miran to Khandesh to ascertain the exact state of affairs and to remove any doubts which might have crept into the mind of Bahadur Khan.

The ambassador proceeded to Khandesh and ascertained that when Bahadur Khan succeeded Raja Ali

Khan, he was a prisoner in the fort of Asir, since it was the established custom among the rulers of Khandesh that the reigning potentate kept his sons, brothers, and other relations in confinement, to guard against attempts upon the throne, so that these unhappy persons, with their wives and families, passed all their lives in confinement. Bahadur Khan had spent nearly thirty years in prison and knew nothing whatever of the ways of the world or the business of government. When he came out of prison and the title of ruler devolved upon him, he plunged recklessly into dissipation. No trace of the tact and nobility which had distinguished Raja Ali Khan was to be found in him. Unmindful of his obligations and obedience to the Imperial throne, he showed no gratitude and sent no tribute, nor did his craven spirit entertain one thought of avenging his father. When this became known to the emperor, he remembered the loyalty and devotion of the late raja, and sent Miran Sadr-i Jahan to give good counsel to the young prince.

Miran proceeded to Asir, where Bahadur Khan at first received him with great respect and honour, and acknowledged the allegiance and duty he owed to the emperor. The envoy, on his side, gave him good counsel and advice, and endeavoured to excite in him a spirit of loyalty. But fate was against the young ruler; he paid but little heed to good counsel and persisted in his own perverse conduct. Sometimes he said he would go to see Akbar; at others he said that suspicions had been aroused in his mind by people's talk which would not allow him to make this visit at present; but he promised to send his son with suitable offerings, if the emperor would graciously direct him to do so. After a while he declared that when all the dependents of the Imperial throne should have been confirmed in their places and he should be able to throw off his feelings of shame, he would proceed in person to pay his respects to the emperor. These excuses proceeded either from his wavering disposition or from a settled design to act treacherously. When Miran, the envoy, found that his representations had no effect upon Bahadur, he communicated the result to the emperor. This roused great anger in the breast of Akbar and was the cause of his sending Shaikh Farid Bokhari to Khandesh.

On the 14th of Sha'ban, while the Imperial camp was at Dhar, Shaikh Farid, the paymaster-general, received orders to lead a considerable force against the fort of Asir. His instructions were to reassure and advise Bahadur Khan. If he proved tractable, he was to be brought to the presence of the emperor; if not, Shaikh Farid was to invest the fort of Asir and reduce it with all possible speed. The Imperial officers were eager to proceed on this service, partly out of zeal in the service of the emperor, partly from the wish to serve under Farid; and with a select force the Shaikh Farid crossed the Narbada, seeking to get information about the enemy. He then learned that the forces of Bahadur Khan were under the command of Sadat Khan, son-in-law of the late Raja Ali Khan, who had been the greatest and the most trusted of all the royal servants.

He had been sent towards Sultanpur and Nandurbar to make a diversion against the Imperial forces in that quarter. It was resolved to detach a force to watch this party, while the remainder marched through Khandesh. On arriving at Gharkol, a humble and submissive letter was brought from Bahadur Khan, recounting the services of his ancestors and volunteering to send his son with suitable offerings to the emperor. He also made excuses for his conduct and solicited the kind intercession of Shaikh Farid to avert the consequences of his faults. The Shaikh sent this letter to the emperor and waited for an answer. Akbar sent a gracious reply, offering to forgive his transgressions and to receive him into favour if he would hasten to pay his allegiance.

Marching forward, the army passed over the summit of Sabalgarh and arrived on the confines of Khandesh. Miran had previously advised that the force should be sent to Burhanpur, lest its advance upon Asir should drive Bahadur Khan to desperation. But when this opinion was represented to the emperor, he gave orders that no attention was to be paid to it, and that the army was not to go to Burhanpur, but was to march direct to Asir and invest the place. Accordingly, it advanced to within two or three leagues of the fortress.

On arriving there, it was learned that Miran and Peshrau Khan, who had also been sent by the emperor to Bahadur, after alternately trying persuasion and menace, were unable to make any impression upon him, and had retired from Asir to Burhanpur. From thence they reported the failure of their mission and left the emperor to determine what was best to be done. On the 21st of Sha'ban the emperor proceeded to Mandu, and when Shaikh Farid came near Asir, Bahadur Khan sent him another letter, containing the same appeals for merciful consideration and offering the same excuses as he had made before. In reply, he was reminded how the kings of the Deccan had united their armies and had made war upon the emperor's allies, and how Raja Ali had fallen fighting bravely and loyally upon the Imperial side. The emperor was now resolved upon revenging his death, and, with God's help, would annex the territories of all the three kings to the Imperial dominions. Bahadur Khan's duty, therefore, was to join the army with his followers without delay, and to take revenge for his father's blood—not to be a thorn in the way and to say to the emperor, "First strike me, and then the murderers of my father." But fortune had turned her back upon the family, and the graceless Bahadur would listen to no reason or expostulation.

The rulers of Khandesh were of the Faruki tribe, and the family had held rule in the country for more than two hundred years. An ancestor who had served in the Deccan as a soldier, being aggrieved, left that country and went to Khandesh, which was then held by different land-holders and rajas. He came to a village which pleased him, and there a dog which accompanied him set off in pursuit of a hare, but the hare turned round and attacked the dog. This unusual exhibition of courage greatly impressed him, and he thought that the land where such a sight could be seen must be fertile in valour and daring, so he resolved to take up his abode there. He expressed his wish to the land-holder of the place, but it was refused. Afterward he seized an opportunity of seeking assistance from the King of Delhi, and, having collected some of his brethren, he overpowered the land-holder and took possession of the village. He extended his power over other villages around, and in the end he was master of several sub-districts and commander of an armed force.

When he died, his authority descended to his grandson, who saw how valuable a fortress would be as a place of safety for his family and dependents. Asir, which is situated on the top of a hill, was at that time an inhabited place. He contrived by various stratagems to obtain this place from the land-holder who possessed it, and fortified it strongly. He then assumed the name of ruler, and at length the whole country of Khandesh, about 150 leagues in length and fifty in breadth, came under his sway. These rulers acted so wisely and carefully that the kings of Delhi did not interfere with them. When the government came to Raja Ali Khan, he showed himself a man of great administrative powers, and it is probable that no one of the dynasty had been his equal in intelligence and ability. People of neighbouring and distant countries had been induced by his just and generous rule to take up their abode in his country. Among the best proofs of his intelligence was his loyalty to the Imperial throne, his obedience, and the magnificence of his offerings, in all which he excelled the other princes of the region.

A TYPE OF INDIAN HILL FORT.

His successor, Bahadur Khan, had none of his ability, and advice was thrown away upon him. The line was drawing to a close and fortune had averted her face. Shaikh Farid invested the fort and reported the fact to the emperor, who sent him reinforcements, and himself passed over the Narbada on his way to superintend the siege. On the 4th of Ramazan the new year of the emperor occurred, and his Majesty halted three days to celebrate the festival. The march of the Imperial force was then resumed.

Letters now arrived from Shaikh Abu-l-fazl, who was coming from the Deccan with the elephants and valuable effects of the late prince, and who announced his arrival at Burhanpur. He had received orders to join Shaikh Farid and to concert measures with him for the punishment of the recusant prince. On the 4th of Farwardin the army marched and encamped two leagues from the fort of Asir, because on that side there was no ground nearer the fort which was fit for a camp. Baz Bahadur Uzbek and Karabeg were sent forward immediately to select positions for the trenches and for the encampment of the besiegers.

On their return they reported that they had never seen in any country a fort like this; for however long an army might press the siege, nothing but the extraordinary good fortune of the emperor could effect its capture. Old soldiers and men who had travelled into distant lands, men who had seen the fortresses of Iran and Turan, of Rum, Europe, and of the whole habitable world, had never beheld the equal of this. It was situated on a high and strong hill, and three smaller hills, each having a fort, stood around it, like a halo round the moon. The ways of entrance and exit were difficult to discover. There was no other hill near it commanding it, and no way of approach. All around was level ground, and there were no trees or jungle to serve as cover. All the time the country had been held by the dynasty, each prince, as he succeeded, did his best to keep the place in repair, to add to its strength, or to increase its stores. It was impossible to conceive a stronger fortress, or one more amply supplied with artillery, warlike stores, and provisions. Were the fortress placed upon level ground, its reduction would be difficult; but such a hill, such a well-secured fortress, and such artillery were not to be found in any one place on the face of the earth.

After the capture of the fortress accounts were taken of the munitions. Of pieces of artillery, small and great, there were more than 1300, besides some which were disused. The balls varied in weight from nearly two *mans* (160 lbs.) down to a *sīr* (2 lbs.) or a half *sīr*. There were great numbers of mortars, and also many catapults, each of which threw stones of 1000 or 2000 *mans*. On every bastion there were large iron cauldrons, in each of which twenty or thirty *mans* of oil could be boiled and poured down upon the assailants in case of assault. No account was taken of the muskets. Of provisions of all sorts, wines, medicines, aromatic roots, and of everything required for the use of man, there was vast abundance. When, after a protracted siege of eleven months, the place fell into the hands of the Imperial army, the quantities of grain, oil, and the like, which remained after some thousands of men had been fed during the siege, seemed as if the stores had never been touched. The stores of ammunition were such that thousands of *mans* were left, although the quantity consumed had been enormous, since throughout the siege a constant firing had been kept up night and day, with object and without object, so that in the dark nights of the rainy season no man dared to raise his head, and even a demon would not move about.

There were also large chambers full of powder. There were no springs of water in the fortress; but there were two or three immense reservoirs, in which rain water was collected and stored from year to year, and which amply sufficed for the requirements of the garrison. In the dwelling of each officer of importance there was a separate reservoir, containing a sufficient supply of pure water for his household. Nor had all this preparation been made for the occasion; it had been kept up from the founding of the fortress. The rulers of the country had incessantly cared for the strengthening and provisioning of the fort, more especially as regarded artillery. The revenues of several sub-districts were specially and separately assigned to keep up the supply of artillery, so that the officers of the department had independent sources for maintaining its efficiency. The population in the fortress was like that of a city, for it was full of men of every kind. After the surrender the inhabitants came out, and there was a continuous throng night and day for a week.

The houses of the chiefs were fine lofty buildings, and there were open spaces, gardens, and fountains. In the walls of the fort, which were of great thickness, chambers and rooms were constructed for the officers of the artillery, where, during all seasons, they could live in comfort and keep up a fire of cannon and musketry. The fortress had one gate, and outside this gate there was another fort called Kamargarh, the walls of which were joined on both sides to the great fort. This was looked upon as an outwork and was held by inferior ranks of men, such as musketeers and archers. Below this fort, but still on an elevated spot, was another fort called Malgarh, which also was very strong. In comparison with the fortress, it seemed at the bottom of the earth; but compared with the surface of the ground, it appeared to be half-way up to the sky. This being the most advanced of the works, great care had been taken to strengthen it with guns and other implements. Below this was an inhabited place called Takhati, as large as a city. In short, the fortress was one of the wonders of the world, and it is impossible to convey an idea of it to any one who has not seen it.

Shaikh Farid, after collecting all the available information about the fortress, wrote a description of it to Akbar and devoted himself to devising a plan for its capture. As the actual strength of the place was not fully known to the emperor, envious men represented its reduction as being an easy matter, and thus vexed him. A letter at length arrived from the camp, announcing the emperor's intention to come and examine matters with his own eyes. About the same time Shaikh Abu-l-fazl arrived from Burhanpur and encamped three or four leagues from Asir, as he was hastening to join the emperor. He sent to inform Shaikh Farid of his presence, and the Shaikh set off to see him. He had gone but a little way when he remembered that Bahadur had promised to see him next day; so he stopped and returned to camp. On the following day Bahadur came down from the fort to meet the Shaikh, and his spies busied themselves in observing all they could. It so happened that on that day a letter was coming from the emperor and the Shaikh mounted to go and meet it, but just as he was starting, his spies brought him word that the cavalcade was approaching. Although Shaikh Farid had with him a large force of horse and foot, musketeers, rocket-men, and elephants, the matter seemed to him important, and he was apprehensive that there was some design against him. So he halted where he was and sent a messenger to Shaikh Abu-l-fazl, to say that he should not come to see him that day, as circumstances prevented him. Shaikh Farid sent messengers to reassure Bahadur, and he came with a large escort to the Shaikh's tent and had an interview with him. Every argument was used to induce him to make his submission to the emperor, and as he had no answer to give, he merely shook his head. At length he returned to his old excuse of being afraid and, rejecting all advice, he returned to the fortress. Some men have maintained that the Shaikh ought to have made him prisoner at this meeting, but resort to subterfuge and want of faith and truth never prove successful. Besides this, Bahadur had with him a force sufficient to resist the weak army of the Shaikh. Next day the Shaikh went to visit Shaikh Abu-l-fazl at his camp, three or four leagues from the fortress, where the meeting with Bahadur was discussed and a report sent off to Akbar.

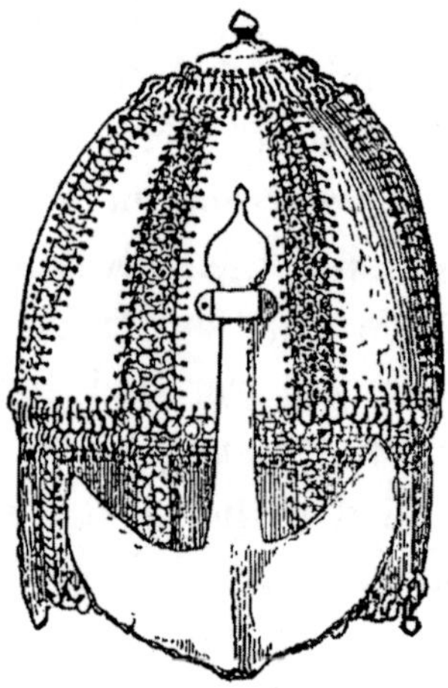

MOGHUL CAVALRY HELMET.

All expectation of Bahadur's submission now being given up, Abu-l-fazl, who had waited to see the result of the interview, proceeded to join the emperor. Having first directed his attention to occupying the country, closing the roads, blocking the way into and out of the fortress, forming the trenches, and preparing other matters connected with the siege, Shaikh Farid sent a detachment to Burhanpur to arrest the officers of Bahadur and to occupy the city. On arriving there, however, it was found that the governor had already made his submission to the emperor. Some experienced officers thought it desirable that a force should be stationed there, and Shaikh Farid finally decided that one thousand horse should be stationed between Burhanpur and Asir. This force took up a position about two leagues from the fortress and cut off all communication between it and the city. Next day Shaikh Abu-l-barakat, brother of Shaikh Abu-l-fazl, joined the besieging force with the elephants and artillery which had been sent under his command. The army now removed to a more favourable position, and it was resolved to form trenches in every suitable place near the fort and to close the roads and entrances. Another letter was received from Bahadur Khan, to which Shaikh Farid replied, but the former trusted in the strength of his fort, and thought that its height and strength were such that no mortal force could take it.

One day when the commander rode toward the fort to examine it, a large gun was fired at him, whereupon, it is related, some of the battlements of the tower on which it was placed fell down, and the gun itself also fell. This was received as a good omen by the Imperial army. Miran Sadr-i Jahan, who had returned to the emperor, now came back, charged with an Imperial message. Next day Miyan Sayyid went round and looked after many things in the construction of the trenches, so that they might afford protection to the men and enable them to stay there day and night. The mind of Akbar was intent upon this undertaking. Letters constantly arrived from him with instructions and urgent directions. Every day some one of his officers came to inspect and report upon the business of the siege.

Having received orders to wait upon the emperor, Shaikh Farid proceeded on the 18th to the royal camp at Burganw, seven or eight leagues from Asir. He was received very kindly and related all the details of the siege. He remained there the next day, and on the following day the Imperial camp moved towards Asir. On the 21st of Farwardin, or 25th of Ramazan, it reached the city of Burhanpur, and the emperor took up his abode in the palace of the old rulers. Intent upon the siege, he then marched on, attended by numerous amirs, and arrived under the fort on the 3d of Shawwal. Shaikh Farid then received orders to attend to his own duties as paymaster-general and wait upon his Majesty, and to appoint the other amirs to the direction of the trenches, so that he might be ready, upon emergency, to lead a force in any direction.

The trenches were then allotted to the different amirs: the first to Khan-i Azam, another to Nawab Asaf Khan, and another to Mirza Jani Beg of Tatta. A fourth trench was placed by Shaikh Farid in charge of his brethren and adherents, and having examined it carefully, he gave it into their charge, while he himself proceeded with a chosen force to attend upon the emperor. It was impossible to dig mines or construct covered ways, and the men in each trench accordingly endeavoured to bring the investment as close as possible. At the end of the month, Azam Khan and Asaf Khan reported that the garrison kept up a fire from different kinds of guns all night and day, with object and without object, necessary and unnecessary, and that the besiegers endured it with great bravery.

In the early days of Zi-al-ka'da, Bahadur sent out

of the fortress sixty-four elephants, along with his mother and son, to the emperor and begged forgiveness of his offences. The emperor replied that if he desired pardon, he must come out at once to make submission, and trust to the emperor's mercy. On the 16th of Zi-al-hijja, a sortie was made, in which many of the garrison lost their lives in a desperate struggle. When they were driven back, a little hill called Koriya fell into the hands of the besiegers. This eminence is so close to the fortress as to have command over it. The besiegers then saw that, by occupying this commanding position and by getting possession of another which was strongly fortified, they might overawe the garrison. The former masters of the place had seen the importance of this position and had scarped the rock so that no one could climb up, but, after hard fighting, the place was finally carried.

On the 21st of Safar, news arrived of the capture of Ahmadnagar on the 18th. The fortress had long been defended by Chand Bai, the sister of Nizam-al-mulk, and when formerly besieged, dissensions among the Imperial amirs averted its capture, but Prince Daniyal, assisted by some of the great amirs, had taken it by assault. The siege of Asir had now been carried on for nearly six months and a constant fire had been kept up without effect, when Khan-khanan thought that mining must be resorted to, and the other amirs coinciding with him, a mine was formed. It was charged with 180 *mans* of gunpowder and was exploded on the 20th of Shahryur, in the 45th year of the reign. A bastion was blown up with seventy or eighty cubits of the wall. Khan-khanan, Raja Jagannath, and the other amirs exerted themselves to incite their troops, and gave orders that the troops were to rush in and finish the work directly after the explosion. This order was duly executed, and a force under Yusuf Khan scaled the wall, by means of a mound, in another place. The assailants pressed on, and after a severe fight, in which a thousand of the besiegers fell, the fortress was captured.

A few days after, Bahadur sent Sadat Khan and Shaikh Pir Muhammad Husain, two of his chief men, to the emperor, with ten elephants and an entreaty for forgiveness. Two days later, Shaikh Pir Muhammad was sent back into the fortress and Sadat Khan was kept as the guest of Shaikh Farid. The escort which had come out with him was ordered to return with Pir Muhammad; but the men, about a hundred in number, declared that they would not return into the fortress and become prisoners in Asir. Permission to remain was given to those who could give some bail that they would not run away, otherwise they were to be put in confinement. In the end some found the required bail, and some went back into the fortress.

Among the causes which brought about the surrender of the fortress was the impurity of the atmosphere, which engendered two diseases. One was paralysis of the lower extremities from the waist downwards, which deprived the sufferer of the power of motion; the other was weakness of sight. These maladies greatly distressed and discouraged the men of the garrison, so that men of all ranks and degrees were of one mind and voice in urging Bahadur to capitulate. At their instance he wrote to the emperor offering to surrender, and thus the siege was ended.

When Bahadur came out, the emperor held a grand darbar, at which all the great men were present, and Bahadur was amazed at the splendour and state. Mukarrib Khan and several other of Bahadur's nobles were sent into the fortress in advance of Shaikh Abu-l-fazl to inform the garrison of the surrender and to demand the keys. When they approached, Mukarrib Khan's father mounted the top of the fort and reviled him for having thrown his master into bonds and surrendered the fort. Unable to endure his abuse, the son stabbed himself two or three times in the abdomen, and a few days afterwards he died. On the 17th of Safar the royal forces were admitted and the keys were given up. Khan-khanan, who had come from Ahmadnagar, went into the fortress and placed the royal seal on the treasure and warlike stores, which were then placed in charge of responsible officers.

On the 8th of Sha'ban, the emperor bestowed great honours on Shaikh Abu-l-fazl, including a banner and kettle-drums; and a hundred amirs were placed under his orders to assist in the subjugation of the Deccan. Khan-khanan was sent to Ahmadnagar, and the general conquest of the Deccan was committed to him. The emperor went in and inspected the fortress. All the treasures and effects of Bahadur Khan, which had been collected by his ancestors during two hundred years, were brought out, and the wives and women of Bahadur, two hundred in number, were presented. The emperor stayed in the place three days, and then proceeded to Burhanpur, while on the 28th of Shawwal all the country of the Deccan, Birar, Khandesh, Malwa, and Gujarat were placed under the rule of Prince Daniyal.

APPENDIX II

IBRAHIM KHAN'S CHRONICLE OF THE MARATHAS

This brief account of the Marathas, written by a native of Hindustan in the latter part of the eighteenth century, is of value because of the clear presentation it gives of certain important historical events in the author's own time, and it serves as a useful supplement to the foregoing sixth and seventh chapters in this volume.

The author, Ibrahim Khan Bahadur, was an illustrious Nawab, or nabob, although he modestly calls himself "the humblest of slaves," and says that he wrote his chronicle "as a volume of warning for men of sagacity." He compiled the work at the time when Lord Cornwallis, of American Revolutionary distinction, was serving as Governor-General of India under George the Third, and he eulogizes Cornwallis in flattering terms.

The book was translated for Sir H. M. Elliot by Major Fuller, and the extracts here presented are from his rendering, with some unimportant omissions and modifications. — EDITOR.

BE it not hidden that in the language of the people of the Deccan these territories and their dependencies are called "Dihast," and the inhabitants of the region are styled "Marathas." The Maratha dialect is adopted exclusively by these classes, and the chieftainship of the Marathas is centred in the Bhonsla tribe. The lineage of the Bhonslas is derived from the Udaipur Rajas, who bear the title of Rana; and the first

SIVAJI, THE FOUNDER OF THE MARATHA POWER.
From Lord Egerton's Indian Armour.

of these, according to popular tradition, was one of the descendants of Naushirwan. At the time when the holy warriors of the army of Islam subverted the realms of Iran, Naushirwan's descendants were scattered in every direction; and one of them, having repaired to Hindustan, was promoted to the dignity of a Raja. In a word, one of the Rana's progeny afterwards quitted the territory of Udaipur, in consequence of the menacing and disordered aspect of his affairs, and having proceeded to the country of the Deccan, fixed his abode in the Carnatic. The chiefs of the Deccan, regarding the majesty of his family with respect and reverence, entered into the most amicable relations with him. His descendants separated into two families; one the Aholias, the other the Bhonslas.

Sahuji, or Shahji of the Bhonslas, was first enrolled among the number of Nizam Shah's retainers, but afterwards entered into the service of Ibrahim Adil Shah, who was the ruler of the Konkan. In return for the faithful discharge of his duties, he received as an annuity the lands and rents of the sub-districts of Poona and other localities, where he made a permanent settlement after the manner of the *zamīndārs*, or land-holders. Towards the close of his life, having attained the high honour of serving the Emperor Jahangir, he was constantly in attendance on him, while his son Sivaji stayed on his estates. As Ibrahim Adil Shah for the space of two years was threatened with impending death, great disorder and confusion prevailed in his territories from the long duration of his illness; and the troops and retainers, whom he had stationed here and there for the purpose of garrisoning the forts and protecting the frontier of the Konkan, abandoned themselves to neglect in consequence of their master's indisposition.

Ultimately, the Emperor Aurangzib, the bulwark of religion, resolved upon proceeding to the Deccan, and in the year 1093 A. H. (1682 A. D.) bestowed fresh lustre

MEKKA GATE AT AURANGABAD.

on the city of Aurangabad by the favour of his august presence. For a period of twenty-five years he strove to subvert the Maratha rule; but as several valiant chieftains displayed the utmost zeal and activity in upholding their dynasty, their extermination could not be satisfactorily accomplished. Towards the close of his Majesty's lifetime, a truce was concluded with the Marathas on condition that three per cent. out of the revenues drawn from the imperial dominions in the Deccan should be allotted to them for the maintenance of the *sar-dēsh-muk*, or head of the district-chiefs; and accordingly Ahsan Khan, commonly called Mir Malik, set out from the threshold of royalty with the documents confirming this grant to the Marathas, in order that, after the treaty had been duly ratified, he might bring the chiefs of that tribe to the court of the monarch of the world. However, before he had had time to deliver these documents into their custody, a royal mandate was issued, directing him to return and bring back the papers in question with him. About this time, his Majesty Aurangzib Alamgir hastened to the eternal gardens of Paradise, at which period his successor Shah Alam (Bahadur Shah) was gracing the Deccan with his presence. The latter settled ten per cent. out of the produce belonging to the peasantry on the Marathas for the *sar-dēsh-muk*, and furnished them with the necessary documents confirming the grant.

When Shah Alam returned from the Deccan to the metropolis, Daud Khan remained behind to officiate for "Amir of amirs" Zu-l Fikar Khan in the government of the provinces. He cultivated a good understanding with the Marathas, and concluded an amicable treaty on the following footing, that in addition to the above-mentioned grant of a tithe for the *sar-dēsh-muk*, a fourth of whatever amount was collected in the country should be their property, while the other three-fourths should be paid into the royal exchequer. This system of division was accordingly put in practice; but no regular deed granting the fourth share, which in the dialect of the Deccan is called *chauth*, was delivered to the Marathas. When Muhammad Farrukhsiyar sat as emperor on the throne of Delhi, he entertained the worst suspicions against Said Husain Ali Khan, the chief of the Barha Sayyids. He dismissed him to a distance from his presence by appointing him to the control of the province of the Deccan. On reaching his destination, the latter applied himself rigorously to the task of organizing the affairs of that kingdom, but royal letters were incessantly despatched to the address of the chief of the Marathas, and more especially to Raja Sahu, urging him to persist in hostilities with Husain Ali.

In the year 1129 A. H. (1717 A. D.), by the intervention of Muhammad Anwar Khan Burhanpuri and Sankaraji Malhar, he concluded a peace with the Marathas, on condition that they would refrain from committing depredations and robberies, and would always maintain eighteen thousand horsemen out of their tribe wholly at the service of the Nizam of the Deccan. At the time that this treaty was ratified, he sealed and delivered the documents confirming the grant of the fourth of the revenues and the *sar-dēsh-mukhī* of the province of the Deccan, as well as the proceeds of the Konkan and other territories, which were designated as their ancient dominions. At the same period Raja Sahu appointed Balaji, son of Basu Nath, who belonged to the class of Konkani Brahmans, to be his representative at the Court of the emperor; and in all the districts of the six provinces of the Deccan he appointed two revenue commissioners of his own, one to collect the *sar-dēsh-mukhī*, and the other to receive the fourth share, or *chauth*.

Amīru-l umarā Husain 'Ali, having increased the *mansabs* held by Balaji, the son of Basu Nath, and Sankaraji Malhar, deputed them to superintend the affairs of the Deccan, and sent them to join 'Alim 'Ali Khan. After the death of Balaji, the son of Basu Nath, his son, named Baji Rao, became his successor, and Holkar, who was a servant of Balaji Rao, having urged the steed of daring, at his master's instigation, at full speed from the Deccan towards Malwa, put Giridhar Bahadur, the governor of Malwa, to death on the field of battle. After this occurrence, the government of that province was conferred on Muhammad Khan Bangash; but owing to the turbulence of the Marathas he was unable to restore it to proper order. On his removal from office, the administration of that region was entrusted to Raja Jai Singh Sawai. Unity of faith and religion strengthened the bonds of amity between Baji Rao and Raja Jai Singh; and this circumstance was a source of additional power and influence to the former, insomuch that during the year 1146 (1733 A. D.) he had the audacity to advance and make an inroad into the confines of Hindustan. The grand vizir Itmad-ad-daulah Kamr-ad-din Khan was first selected by the Emperor Muhammad Shah to oppose him, and on the second occasion Muzaffar Khan, the brother of Samsam-ad-daulah Khan-dauran. These two, having entered the province of Malwa, pushed on as far as

Sironj, but Baji Rao returned to the Deccan without hazarding an engagement.

In the second year after this, Baji Rao attempted another invasion of Hindustan, when the vizir Itmad-ad-daulah Kamr-ad-din Khan Bahadur and the Nawab Khan-dauran Khan went forth from Delhi to give him battle. On this occasion several engagements took place, but victory fell to the lot of the vizir; and peace having been ultimately concluded, they both returned to Delhi.

In the third year from the aforesaid date, through the mediation of Khan-dauran Khan Bahadur, the government of Malwa was bestowed on Baji Rao, whereby his power and influence was increased twofold. The Rao in question, having entered Malwa with a numerous force, soon reduced the province to a satisfactory state of order. About the same time he attacked the Raja of Bhadawar, and after putting him to flight, devastated his territory. From thence he sent Pilaji with the view of subduing the kingdom of Antarbed (Doab), which is situated between the Ganges and Jumna. At that very time Nawab Burhan-al-mulk had moved out of his own province, and advanced through Antarbed to the vicinity of Agra. Pilaji therefore crossed the Jumna, and engaged in active hostilities against the Nawab; but having been vanquished in battle, he was forced to take to flight and rejoin Baji Rao. An immense number of his army were drowned while crossing the Jumna; but as for those who were captured or taken prisoners, the Nawab presented each one with two rupees and a cloth, and gave him permission to depart. Baji Rao, becoming downcast and dispirited after meeting with this ignominious defeat, turned his face from that quarter and proceeded towards Delhi.

Samsam-ad-daulah Amir-ul-umara Bahadur, after considerable deliberation, sallied forth from Shahjahanabad with intent to check the enemy; but Baji Rao, not deeming it expedient at the time to kindle the flame of war, retired towards Agra, and the "Amir of amirs," considering himself fortunate enough in having effected so much, re-entered the metropolis. This was the first occasion on which the Marathas extended their aggressions so far as to threaten the environs of the metropolis. Though most of the men in the Maratha army are unendowed with the excellence of noble and illustrious birth, and husbandmen, carpenters, and shopkeepers abound among their soldiery, yet, as they undergo all sorts of toil and fatigue in prosecuting a guerrilla warfare, they prove superior to the lazy and effeminate troops of Hind, who for the most part are of more honourable birth and calling. If this class were to apply their energies with equal zeal to the profession and free themselves from the trammels of indolence, their prowess would excel that of their rivals, for the aristocracy ever possess more spirit than the vulgar herd. The freebooters who form the vanguard of the Maratha forces, and, marching in advance of their main body, ravage the enemy's country, are called *pĭndāras*; the troops who are stationed here and there by way of pickets at a distance from the army for the purpose of keeping a vigilant watch are styled *mati;* and *chhappah* is synonymous in their dialect with a night-attack. Their food consists chiefly of simple cakes, with a little butter and red pepper; and hence it is that, owing to the irascibility of their tempers, gentleness is never met with in their dispositions. The ordinary dress worn by these people comprises a turban, tunic, *selah* (loose mantle), and the *janghiah* (short drawers). Among their horses are many mares, and among the offensive weapons used by this tribe there are but few firearms, most of the men being armed with swords, spears, or arrows instead. The system of military service established among them is this: each man, according to his grade, receives a fixed salary in cash and clothes every year. They call their stables *pāgāh*, and the horsemen who belong to a superior officer are styled *bārgīrs.*

A MARATHA BRAHMAN.

When Baji Rao, in the year 1153 A. H. (1740 A. D.), on the banks of the river Narbada, bore the burden of his existence to the shores of nonentity, his son, Balaji Rao, became his successor, and, after the manner of his father, engaged vigorously in the prosecution of hostilities, the organization and equipment of a large army, and the preparation of all the munitions of war. His son continued to pass his days, sometimes at war, and at other times at peace, with the Nawab Asaf Jah. At length, in the year 1163 (1750 A. D.), Sahu Rao, the successor of Sambhaji, passed away, and the supreme authority departed out of the direct line of the Bhonslas. Balaji Rao selected another individual of that family, in place of Sahu's son, to occupy the post of Raja, and seated him on the throne, while he reserved for himself the entire administration of all the affairs of the kingdom. Having then degraded the ancient chieftains from the lofty position they had held, he denuded them of their dignity and influence, and began aggrandizing the Konkani Brahmans, who were of the same caste as himself. He also constituted his cousin, Sadasheo Rao, commonly called Bhao Rao, his chief agent and prime minister. The individual in question was of acute understanding and thoroughly conversant with the proper method of government. Through the influence of his energetic counsels, many undertakings were constantly brought to a successful issue, the recital of which would lead to too great prolixity. In short, besides holding the fortress of Bijapur, he took possession anew of Daulatabad, the seat of government of the illustrious sovereigns, together with districts yielding six million rupees, after forcibly wresting it out of the hands of Nizam Ali Khan Bahadur. He likewise took into his service Ibrahim Khan Gardi, who had a well-organized train of European artillery with him.

In the year 1171 A. H. (1757-8 A. D.), Ahmad Shah

Abdali came from the country of Kandahar to Hindustan, and on the 7th of Jumad-al-awwal of that year had an interview with the Emperor Alamgir II at the palace of Shahjahanabad; he exercised all kinds of severity and oppression on the inhabitants of that city, and united the daughter of Aazz-ad-din, own brother to his Majesty, in the bonds of wedlock with his own son Timur Shah. After an interval of a month, he set out to coerce Raja Suraj Mal Jat, who, from a distant period, had extended his sway over the province of Agra as far as the environs of the city of Delhi. In three days he captured Balamgarh, situated at a distance of fifteen leagues from Delhi, which was furnished with all the requisites for standing a siege and was well manned by Suraj Mal's followers. After causing a general massacre of the garrison, he hastened towards Mathura, and having razed that ancient sanctuary of the Hindus to the ground, made all the idolaters fall a prey to his relentless sword. He then returned to Agra, and deputed his commander-in-chief, Jahan Khan, to reduce all the forts belonging to the Jat chieftain. At this time a dreadful pestilence broke out with great virulence in the Shah's army, so that he was forced to abandon his intention of chastising Suraj Mal, and unwillingly made up his mind to repair to his own kingdom.

On his return, as soon as he reached Delhi, the Emperor Alamgir went forth with Najib-ad-daulah Bahadur, and had an interview with him on the margin of the Maksudabad Lake, where he preferred sore complaints

DAULATABAD.

against Imad-al-mulk Ghazi-ad-din Khan Bahadur, who was at that time at Farrukhabad, engaged in exciting seditious tumults. The Shah, after forming a matrimonial alliance with the daughter of his late Majesty Muhammad Shah, and investing Najib-ad-daulah with the title of "Amir of amirs" and the dignified post of paymaster-general, set out for Lahore. As soon as he had planted his sublime standard on that spot, he conferred the government of both Lahore and Multạn on his son Timur Shah, and leaving Jahan Khan behind with him, himself proceeded to Kandahar.

Jahan Khan despatched a warrant to Adina Beg Khan, who at that time had taken up his residence at Lakhi Jangal, investing him with the supreme control of the territory of the Doab, along with a robe of investiture of immense value, and adopted the most conciliatory measures towards him, whereupon the latter, esteeming this amicable attention as a mark of good fortune, applied himself zealously to the proper administration of the Doab. When Jahan Khan, however, summoned him to his presence, he did not consider it to his advantage to wait upon him; so, quitting the territory of the Doab, he retired into the hill-country. After this occurrence, Jahan Khan appointed a person named Murad Khan to the charge of the Doab, and sent Sarbuland Khan and Sarfaraz Khan, of the Abdali tribe, along with him to assist him. Adina Beg Khan, having united the Sikh nation to his own forces, advanced to give battle to Murad Khan, when Sarbuland Khan quaffed the cup of martyrdom on the field of action, and Murad Khan and Sarfaraz Khan, seeing no resource left them but flight, returned to Jahan Khan, and the Sikhs ravaged all the districts of the Doab.

As soon as active hostilities were commenced between Najib-ad-daulah and Imad-al-mulk, the latter set out from Farrukhabad towards Delhi to oppose the former, and forwarded letters to Balaji Rao and his cousin Bhao, soliciting aid and inviting the Maratha army to espouse his cause. Bhao, who was always cherishing plans in his head for national aggrandizement, counselled Balaji Rao to despatch an army for the conquest of the territories of Hindustan, which he affirmed to be then, as it were, an assembly unworthy of reverence, and a rose devoid of thorns.

In 1171 A. H. (1757-8 A. D.), Raghunath Rao, a brother of Balaji Rao, accompanied by Malhar Rao Holkar, Shamsher Bahadur, and Jayaji Sindhia, started from the Deccan towards Delhi at the head of a gallant and irresistible army to subdue the dominions of Hindustan. As soon as they reached Agra, they turned off to Shahjahanabad in company with Imad-al-mulk the vizir, who was the instigator of the irruption made by this torrent of destruction. After a sanguinary engagement, they ejected Najib-ad-daulah from the city of Delhi and consigned the management of the affairs of government to the care of Imad-al-mulk, the vizir.

Raghunath Rao and the rest of the Maratha chiefs set out from Delhi towards Lahore at the solicitation of Adina Beg Khan, of whom mention has been briefly made above. After leaving the suburbs of Delhi, they arrived first at Sirhind, where they fought an action with Abd-as-samad Khan, who had been installed in the government of that place by the Abdali Shah Ahmad, and took him prisoner. Turning away from thence, they pushed on to Lahore and got ready for a conflict with Jahan Khan, who was stationed there. The latter, however, being alarmed at the paucity of his troops in comparison with the multitude of the enemy, resolved at once to seek safety in flight. Accordingly, in the month of Sha'ban, 1171 A. H. (April, 1758 A. D.), he pursued the road to Kabul with the utmost speed, accompanied by Timur Shah, and made a present to the enemy of the heavy baggage and property that he had accumulated during his administration of that region. The Maratha chieftains followed in pursuit of Timur Shah as far as the river Attok, and then retraced their steps to Lahore. This time the Marathas extended their sway up to Multan. As the rainy season had commenced, they delivered over the province of Lahore to Adina Beg Khan on his promising to pay a tributary offering of 7,500,000 rupees, and made up their minds to return to the Deccan, being anxious again to behold their beloved families at home.

On reaching Delhi in the course of their return, they made straight for their destination, after leaving one of their warlike chieftains, named Janku, at the head of a formidable army in the vicinity of the metropolis. It chanced that in the year 1172 A. H.

(1758-9 A. D.) Adina Beg Khan passed away, whereupon Jankuji entrusted the government of the province of Lahore to a Maratha called Sama, whom he sent thither. He also appointed Sadik Beg Khan, one of Adina Beg Khan's followers, to the administration

THE RIVER ATTOK.

of Sirhind, and gave the management of the Doab to Adina Beg Khan's widow. Sama, after reaching Lahore, applied himself to the task of government, and pushed on his troops as far as the river Attok. In the meanwhile, Imad-al-mulk, the vizir, caused Shah Alamgir II to suffer martyrdom in retaliation for an ancient grudge, and placed the son of Muhi-as-sunnat, son of Kam-Bakhsh, son of Aurangzib Alamgir, on the throne of Delhi.

Datta Sindhia, Jankuji's uncle, about that time formed the design of invading the kingdom of the Rohillas; whereupon Najib-ad-daulah and other Rohilla chiefs, becoming cognizant of this fact and perceiving the image of ultimate misfortune reflected in the mirror of the very beginning, wrote numerous letters to the Abdali Shah, and used every persuasion to induce him to come to Hindustan. The Shah, who was vexed at heart because Timur Shah and Jahan Khan had been compelled to take to flight, and was brooding over plans of revenge, accounted this friendly overture a signal advantage and set himself at once in motion.

Datta, in company with his nephew Janku, after crossing the Jumna, advanced against Najib-ad-daulah, and Imad-al-mulk, the vizir, hastened to Datta's support, agreeably to his request. As the number of the Maratha troops amounted to nearly 80,000 horse, Najib-ad-daulah, finding his strength inadequate to risk an open battle, threw up intrenchments at Sakartal, one of the places belonging to Antarbed (the Doab), situated on the bank of the river Ganges, and there held himself in readiness to oppose the enemy. As the rainy season presented an insurmountable obstacle to Datta's movements, he was forced to suspend military operations, and in the interim Najib-ad-daulah despatched several letters to Nawab Shuja-ad-daulah, begging his assistance.

The Nawab, urged by the promptings of valour and

gallantry, started from Lucknow in the height of the rains, which fell with greater violence than in ordinary years, and having with the utmost spirit and resolution traversed the intervening roads, which were all in a wretched muddy condition, made Shahabad the site of his camp. Till the conclusion of the rainy season, however, he was unable to unite with Najib-ad-daulah, owing to the overflowing of the river Ganges.

No sooner had the rains come to an end, than one of the Maratha chieftains, who bore the appellation of Govind Pandit, forded the stream at Datta's command with a party of 20,000 cavalry, and allowed no portion of Chandpur and many other populous places to escape conflagration and plunder. He then betook himself to the spot where Sad-allah Khan, Dundi Khan, and Hafiz Rahmat Khan had assembled, after having risen up in arms and quitted their abodes to afford succour to Najib-ad-daulah. These three, finding themselves unable to cope with him, took refuge in the forests on the Kamaun hills.

Nawab Shuja-ad-daulah, being apprised of this circumstance, mounted the fleet steed of resolution, and in Rabi-al-awwal, 1173 A. H. (Oct.-Nov. 1759 A. D.), taking his troops resembling the stars in his train, he repaired on the wings of speed to Chandpur, close to the locality where Najib-ad-daulah was stationed. As Govind Pandit had reduced the latter's force as well as his companions to great straits by cutting off their supply of provisions, Nawab Shuja-ad-daulah Bahadur despatched 10,000 cavalry, consisting of Moghuls and others, under the command of Mirza Najaf Khan Bahadur, Mir Bakar Himmati, and other leaders, to attack the Pandit's camp. He afterwards also sent off Anupgar Gosain and Raj Indar Gosain in rear of these. The leaders in question having fought with becoming gal-

LANDING GHATS ALONG THE GANGES.

lantry and performed the most valiant deeds, succeeded in routing the enemy. Out of the whole of Govind Pandit's force, 200 were left weltering in blood and as many more were captured alive, while a vast number were overwhelmed in the waters of the Ganges. Immense booty also fell into the hands of the victors, comprising every description of valuable goods, together with horses and cattle. Govind Pandit, who, after suffering this total defeat, had escaped from the field of battle across the river Ganges, gave himself up to despair and took to a precipitate flight. As soon as this intelligence reached the ears of Hafiz Rahmat Khan and the rest of the Rohilla chieftains, they sallied forth from the forests of Kaman, and repaired to Nawab Shuja-ad-daulah's camp. Meanwhile Najib-ad-daulah was released from the perils and misfortunes of his position.

Nawab Shuja-ad-daulah Bahadur assembled the Rohilla chiefs and offered them advice in the following strain: "The enemy has an innumerable army, his military prowess is formidable, and he has gained possession of most of the districts in your territory; it is therefore better for you to make overtures for peace." Every one, both high and low, applauded the Nawab's judicious counsel and voted that pacific negotiations should be immediately begun with Datta; but the truce had not yet been established on a secure basis, when the news of Ahmad Shah Abdali's approach and of his arrival on this side of Lahore astonished the ears of all. Datta, with the arrogance that ever filled his head, would not allow the preliminaries of peace to be brought to a conclusion; but haughtily discarding the amicable relations that he was in process of contracting, moved with a resolute step along the road to Delhi with a view to encounter the Abdali Shah. He was accompanied at that time by 80,000 horsemen, well armed and equipped.

When the Shah set out from Lahore in the direction of Delhi, he thought to himself that on the direct road between these two places, owing to the passage to and fro of the Maratha troops, it would be difficult to find any thriving villages, and grain and forage would be almost unprocurable. Consequently, in the month of Rabi-al-awwal, 1173 A. H., he crossed the river Jumna and entered Antarbed, whereupon Najib-ad-daulah and the other Rohilla chiefs, whose territories were situated in that kingdom, came to join the Shah. They likewise brought sums of money, as well as grain and provisions, to whatever extent they could procure them, and delivered them over for the Shah's use. Through this cordial support of the Rohilla chiefs, the Shah acquired redoubled strength, and having directed his corps of Durranis, who were employed in the campaign on skirmishing duties, to pursue the ordinary route, and be in readiness for an engagement with Datta, he himself proceeded on his march to the eastward, by way of Antarbed.

A MARATHA HELMET.

On this side too, Datta, travelling with the speed of wind and lightning, conducted his army to Sirhind, where he happened to fall in with the Shah's skirmishing parties. As the Durranis are decidedly superior to the Maratha troops in the rapidity of their evolutions and in their system of predatory warfare, the moment they confronted each other, Datta's army was unable to hold its ground. Being compelled to give way, he retired to Delhi, keeping up a running fight all the way, and took up a position in the plain of Bawali, which lies in the vicinity of Shahjahanabad. At that juncture, Jankuji proposed to his nephew, with haughty pride, that they should try and extricate themselves from their critical situation, and Jankuji at once did exactly what his uncle suggested. In fact, Datta and his troops dismounted from their horses after the manner of the inhabitants of Hind about to sacrifice their lives, and boldly maintained their footing on the field of battle. The Durranis assailed the enemy with arrows, matchlocks, and swords, and so overpowered them as not to allow a single individual to escape in safety from the scene of action. This event took place in Jumad-al-awwal, 1173 A. H. (January, 1760 A. D.).

As soon as this intelligence reached the quick ear of Malhar Rao Holkar, who at that time was staying at Makandara, he consigned the surrounding districts to the flames, and making up his mind, proceeded in extreme haste to Suraj Mal Jat, and importuned that raja to join him in the war against the Durrani Shah. The latter, however, strongly objected to complying with his request, stating that he was unable to advance out of his own territory to engage in hostilities with them, as he had not sufficient strength to risk a pitched battle; and that if the enemy were to make an attack upon him, he would seek refuge within his forts. In the interview, it came to Holkar's knowledge that the Afghans of Antarbed had moved out of their villages with treasure and provisions, with intent to convey them to the Shah's camp, and had arrived as far as Sikandra, which is one of the dependencies of Antarbed, situated at a distance of twenty leagues from Delhi, towards the east. He consequently pursued them with the utmost celerity, and having fallen upon them, delivered them up to indiscriminate plunder and rapine.

The Abdali Shah, having been apprised of this circumstance, deputed Shah Kalandar Khan and Shah Pasand Khan Durrani, at the head of 15,000 horse, to chastise Holkar. The individuals in question, having reached Delhi from Narnaul, a distance of seventy leagues, in twenty-four hours, and having halted during the day to recover from their fatigues, effected a rapid passage across the Jumna, as soon as half the night was over, and by using the utmost expedition succeeded in reaching Sikandra by sunrise. They then encompassed Holkar's army, and made a vast number of his men fall a prey to their relentless swords. Holkar found himself reduced to great straits; he had not even sufficient leisure to fasten a saddle on his horse, but was compelled to mount with merely a saddlecloth under him, and flee for his life. Three hundred more horsemen also followed after him in the same destitute plight, but the remainder of his troops, being completely hemmed in, were either slain or captured, and an immense quantity of property and household goods, as well as numbers of horses, fell into the hands of the Durranis. About this time, too, the Shah arrived at Delhi from Narnaul, and took up his quarters in the city.

In the year 1172 A. H. (1758-9 A. D.), Raghunath

THE JAMI' MASJID AT DELHI.

Rao, the brother of Balaji Rao, after confiding the provinces of Lahore and Multan to Adina Beg Khan, and leaving Jankuji with a formidable army in the vicinity of the metropolis of Delhi, arrived at the city of Poona along with Shamsher Bahadur, Malhar Rao Holkar, and Jayaji Sindhiya. Sadasheo Rao Bhaoji, who was Balaji Rao's cousin, and his chief agent and prime minister, began instituting inquiries as to the receipts and disbursements made during the invasion of

Hind. As soon as it became apparent that after spending the revenue that had been levied from the country and the proceeds arising from the plundered booty, the pay of the soldiery, amounting to about six million rupees, was due, the vain illusion was dissipated from Bhaoji's brain. The latter's dislike to Raghunath Rao, moreover, had now broken into open contumely and discord, and Balaji Rao, vexed and disgusted at finding his own brother despised and disparaged, sent a letter to Bhaoji, declaring that it was essentially requisite for him now to unfurl the banner of invasion in person against Hindustan, and endure the fatigues of the campaign, since he was so admirably fitted for the undertaking. Bhao, without positively refusing to consent to his wishes, managed to evade compliance for a whole year, by having recourse to prevarication and subterfuge.

In the next year (1759-60 A. D.), Biswas Rao, Balaji Rao's eldest son, who was seventeen years old, solicited the command of the army from his father; and though the latter was in reality displeased with his request, yet he sent him off in company with Bhaoji, Malhar Rao, Pilaji Jadaun, Jan Rao Dhamadsari, Shamsher Bahadur, Sabuli Dadaji Rao, Jaswant Rao Bewar, Balwant Rao, Ganesh Rao, and other famous and warlike leaders, together with a force of 35,000 cavalry. Ibrahim Khan Gardi, who was the superintendent of the European artillery, likewise accompanied him. Owing to the extreme sultriness of the hot season, they were obliged to rest every other day, and thus by alternate marches and halts, they at length reached Gwalior.

As soon as the particulars of Datta's death and Holkar's defeat, as well as the rout and spoliation of both their forces, were poured into the ears of Biswas Rao and Bhaoji by the reporters of news and the detailers of intelligence, vast excitement arose, so that a sojourn of two months took place at Gwalior. Malhar Rao Holkar, who had escaped with his life from the battle with the Durranis, and in the mean time had joined Biswas Rao's camp, then started from Gwalior for Shahjahanabad by Bhao's order, at the head of a formidable army, and having reached Agra, took Jankuji Sindhia along with him from thence, and drew near to his destination.

Ahmad Shah Abdali, on ascertaining this news, sallied out from the city of Delhi to encounter him; but the latter, finding himself unable to resist, merely made some dashing excursions to the right and left for a few days, after the guerrilla fashion. As the Shah, however, would never once refrain from pursuing him, he was ultimately forced to make an ignominious retreat back along the road he had come, and having returned to Gwalior, went and rejoined Bhaoji. The rainy season was coming on, so Ahmad Shah crossed the river Jumna, and having encamped at Sikandra, gave instructions to the officers of his army to prepare houses of wood and grass for themselves, in place of tents and pavilions.

Bhao and Biswas Rao marched from Gwalior, after

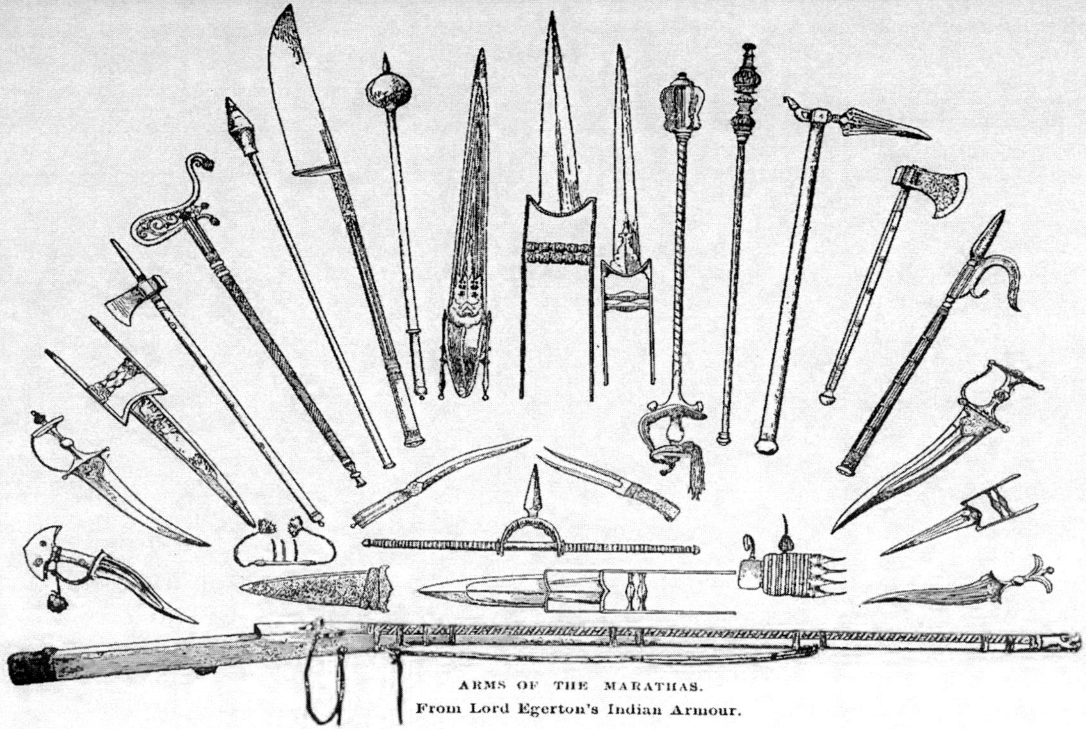

ARMS OF THE MARATHAS.

From Lord Egerton's Indian Armour.

travelling many stages, and traversed long distances, but as soon as they reached Akbarabad, Holkar and Jankuji, at Bhao's instigation, betook themselves to Raja Suraj Mal Jat, and brought him along with them to have an interview with Bhao. The latter went out a league from camp to meet him, and Imad-al-mulk, the vizir, also held a conference with Bhao through Suraj Mal's mediation. Suraj Mal proposed that the campaign should be conducted on the following plan: that they should deposit their extra baggage and heavy guns, together with their female relatives, in the fort of Jhansi, by the side of the river Chambal; and then proceed to wage a predatory and desultory style of warfare against the enemy, as is the usual practice of the Maratha troops; for under these circumstances their own territory would be behind their backs, and a constant supply of provisions would not fail to reach their camp in safety. Bhao and the other leaders, after hearing Suraj Mal's observations, approved of his decision; but Biswas Rao, who was an inexperienced youth, intoxicated with the wine of arrogance, would not follow his advice. Bhao accordingly carried on operations in conformity with Biswas Rao's directions, and set out from Akbarabad towards Delhi with the force that he had at his disposal. On Tuesday, the 9th of Zi-al-hijja, 1173 A. H. (Sept. 23, 1760 A. D.), about the time of rising of the world-illumining sun, he enjoyed the felicity of beholding the fort of Delhi. The command of the garrison there was at that time entrusted to Yakub Ali Khan Bahmanzai, brother to Shah Wali Khan, the prime minister of the Durrani Shah; who, in spite of the multitude of his enemies, would not succumb, and spared no exertions to protect the fort with the few martial spirits that he had with him.

Bhao, conjecturing that the fort of Delhi would be devoid of protection of any garrison, and would therefore, immediately on being besieged, fall under his subjection, went and took up a position near Sadallah Khan's mansion, with a multitude of troops. Ibrahim Khan Gardi, who was a confederate of Bhao and had the superintendence of the European artillery, planted his thundering cannon, with their skilful gunners, opposite the fort on the side of the sandy plain, and having made the battlements of the Octagon Tower and the Asad Burj a mark for his lightning-darting guns, overturned many of the royal edifices. Every day the tumultuous noise of attack on all sides of the fort filled the minds of the garrison with alarm and apprehension. The overflowing of the Jumna presented an insurmountable obstacle to the crossing of the Durrani Shah's army, and hindered it from affording any succour to the besieged. The provisions in the fort were very nearly expended, and Yakub Ali Khan was forced to enter into negotiations for peace. He first removed, with his female relatives and property, from the fort to the domicile of Ali Mardan Khan, and then, having crossed the river Jumna from thence on board a boat, betook himself to the Shah's camp. On the 19th of the aforesaid month and year,

Carved Pillar in Dewan-I-Khas, Fatepur-Sikri.
From a Photograph.

Bhao entered the fort along with Biswas Rao, and took possession of all the property and goods that he could find in the old repositories of the royal family. He also broke in pieces the silver ceiling of the Diwan-i-Khas, from which he extracted so much of the precious metal as to be able to coin 1,700,000 rupees out of it. Narad Shankar Brahmin was then appointed by Bhao to the post of governor of the fort.

The Durrani Shah, after his engagement with Datta, which terminated in the destruction of the latter, had despatched Najib-ad-daulah to the province of Oudh with a conciliatory epistle, which was, as it were, a treaty of friendship, for the purpose of fetching Nawab Shuja-ad-daulah Bahadur. Najab-ad-daulah accordingly betook himself by way of Etawa to Kanauj; and about the same time Nawab Shuja-ad-daulah marched from Lucknow, and made the ferry of Mahdipur, which is one of the places in Etawa situated on this side the river Ganges, the site of his camp. An interview took place in that locality, and as soon as the friendly document had been perused, and the Nawab's heart had been comforted by its sincere promises, he came to the fixed determination of waiting on the Shah, and sent back Raja Beni Bahadur, who at that time possessed greater power and influence than his other followers, to rule as viceroy over the kingdom during his absence. When Nawab Shuja-ad-daulah approached the Shah's army, the prime minister, Shah Wali Khan, hastened out to meet him, and, having brought him along with him in the most courteous and respectful manner, afforded him the gratification, on the 4th of Zi-al-hijja, 1173 A. H. (July 18, 1760 A. D.), of paying his respects to the Shah, and of folding the son of the latter, Timur Shah, in his embrace.

Bhao remained some time in the fort of Shahjahanabad, in consequence of the rainy season, which prevented the horses from stirring a foot, and deprived the cavalry of the power of fighting; he sent a person named Bhawani Shankar Pandit to Nawab Shuja-ad-daulah with the following message: "If it is inconvenient for you to contract an alliance with your friends, you should at least keep aloof from the enemy, and remain perfectly neutral to both parties." The Pandit, having crossed the river Jumna, went to Nawab Shuja-ad-daulah Bahadur, and delivered this message. The latter, after ascertaining its drift, despatched his eunuch Yakut Khan, who was one of the oldest and most confidential servants of his government, in company with Bhawani Shankar Pandit, and returned an answer of this description: "As the Rajas of this empire and the Rohilla chiefs were reduced to the last extremity by the violent aggressions of Raghunath Rao, Datta, Holkar, and their subordinates, they solicited the Abdali Shah to come to Hindustan, with the view of saving themselves from ruin. 'The seed that they sowed has now begun to bear fruit.' Nevertheless, if peace be agreeable to you, from true regard for our ancient friendship, my best endeavours shall be used towards concluding one." Eventually Bhao proposed that as far as Sirhind should be under the Shah's dominion, and all on this side of it should belong to him; but the whole rainy season was spent in negotiation, and no peace was established.

In the interim, Raja Suraj Mal Jat, who discerned the speedy downfall of the Maratha power, having moved with his troops in company with Imad-al-mulk, the vizir, from his position at Sarai Badarpur, which is situated at a distance of six leagues from Delhi on the eastern side, and traversed fifty leagues in one night, without informing Bhao, betook himself to Balamgarh, which is one of his forts.

As the Maratha troops made repeated complaints to Bhao regarding the scarcity of grain and forage, the latter, on the 29th of the month of Safar, 1174 A. H. (Oct. 9, 1760 A. D.), removed Shah Jahan, son of Muhi'u-s Sunnat, son of Kam Bakhsh, son of Aurangzib 'Alamgir, and having seated the illustrious prince, Mirza Jawan Bakht, the grandson of 'Alamgir II, on the throne of Delhi, publicly conferred the dignity of vizir on Shuja-ad-daulah. His object was this, that the Durrani Shah might become averse to and suspicious of the Nawab in question. Leaving Narad Shankar Brahmin, of whom mention has been made above, behind in the fort of Shahjahanabad, he himself set out, with all his partisans and retainers, in the direction of Kunjpura. This place is fifty-four leagues to the west of Delhi, and seven to the north of the sub-district of Karnal, and it is a district the original cultivators of which were the Rohillas.

Bhao, on the 10th of Rabi-al-awway, 1174 A. H. (Oct.

19, 1760), encompassed the fort of Kunjpura with his troops, and subdued it in the twinkling of an eye by the fire of his thundering cannon. Several chiefs were in the fort, one of whom was Abd-as-samad Khan Abdali, governor of Sirhind, who had been taken prisoner by Raghunath Rao in 1170 A. H. (1756-7 A. D.), but had ultimately obtained his release, as was related in the narrative of Adina Beg Khan's proceedings. There were, besides, Kutb Khan Rohilla, Dalil Khan, and Nijabat Khan, all landholders of places in Antarbed, who had been guilty of conveying supplies to the Abdali Shah's camp. After reducing the fort, Bhao made Abd-as-samad Khan and Kutb Khan undergo capital punishment, and kept the rest in confinement; while he allowed Kunjpura itself to be sacked by his predatory hordes.

As soon as this intelligence reached the Shah's ear, the sea of his wrath was deeply agitated; and notwithstanding that the stream of the Jumna had not yet subsided sufficiently to admit of its being forded, a royal edict was promulgated, directing his troops to pay no regard to the current, but cross at once from one bank to the other. As there was no help but to comply with this mandate, on the 16th of the month of Rabi-al-awwal, 1174 A. H. (Oct. 25, 1760 A. D.), near Shahjahanabad, on the road to Pakpat, which is situated fifteen leagues to the north of Delhi, they resigned themselves to fate, and succeeded in crossing. A number were swallowed up by the waves, and a small portion of the baggage and quadrupeds belonging to the army was lost in the passage. As soon as the intelligence reached Bhao's ear, that a party of Durranis had crossed, he sounded the drum of retreat from Kunjpura, and with his force of forty thousand well-mounted and veteran cavalry, and a powerful train of European artillery, under the superintendence of Ibrahim Khan

THE JUMNA AT AGRA.

Gardi, he repaired expeditiously to Panipat, which lies forty leagues from Delhi towards the west.

The Abdali Shah, after crossing the river Jumna at the landing-steps of Pakpat, proceeded in a westerly direction, and commanded that Nawab Shuja-ad-daulah Bahadur and Najib-ad-daulah should pitch their tents on the left of the royal army, and Dundi Khan, Hafiz-al-Mulk, Hafiz Rahmat Khan, and Ahmad Khan Bangash on the right. As Bhao perceived that it was difficult to contend against the Durranis in the open field, by the advice of his counsellors he made a permanent encampment of his troops in the outskirts of the city of Panipat, and having intrenched it all round with his artillery, took up his quarters in this very formidable position.

When the basis of the enemy's power had been overthrown at Panipat, and the surface of the plain had been relieved of the insolent foe, the triumphant champions of the victorious army proceeded eagerly to pillage the Maratha camp, and succeeded in gaining possession of an unlimited quantity of silver and jewels, five hundred enormous elephants, fifty thousand horses, one thousand camels, and two hundred thousand bullocks, with a vast amount of goods and chattels, and a countless assortment of camp equipage. Nearly thirty thousand labourers, too, who drew their origin from the Deccan, fell into captivity. Towards evening the Abdali Shah went out to look at the bodies of the slain, and found great heaps of corpses, and running streams produced by the flood of gore. Thirty-two mounds of slain were counted, and the ditch, protected by artillery, of such immense length that it could contain several hundred thousand of human beings, besides cattle and baggage, was completely filled with dead bodies.

Rao Kashi Nath, on seeing Jankuji, who was a youth of twenty, with a handsome countenance, and at that time had his wounded hand hanging in a sling from his neck, became deeply grieved, and the tears started from his eyes. Jankuji raised his head and exclaimed: "It is better to die with one's friends than to live among one's enemies."

The Nawab, in unison with Shah Wali Khan, solicited the Shah to spare Jankuji's life; whereupon the Shah summoned Barkhurdar Khan, and consulted him on the propriety of the step, to which the Khan in question returned a decided negative. At the same time, one of the Durranis, at Barkhurdar Khan's suggestion, went and cut Jankuji's throat, and buried him under ground inside the very tent in which he was imprisoned.

Shuja-ad-kuli Khan, a powerful and influential servant of the Nawab Shuja-ad-daulah Bahadur, having captured Ibrahim Khan Gardi on the field of battle, kept him with the said Nawab's cognizance in his own tent. No sooner did this intelligence become public than the Durranis began in a body to raise a violent tumult, and clamorously congregating round the door of the Shah's tent, declared that Ibrahim Gardi's neck was answerable for the loss of so many thousands of their fellow countrymen, and that whoever sought to protect him would incur the penalty of their resentment. Nawab Shuja-ad-daulah, feeling that one seeking refuge cannot be slain, prepared for a contest with the Durrani forces, whereupon there ensued a frightful disturbance. At length, Shah Wali Khan took Nawab Shuja-ad-daulah aside privately, and addressing him in a friendly and affectionate tone, proposed that he should deliver up Ibrahim Khan Gardi to him, for the sake of appeasing the wrath of the Durranis; and after a week, when their evil passions had been allayed, he would restore to him the individual entrusted to his care. In short, Shah Wali Khan, having obtained him from the Nawab, applied a poisonous plaster to his wounds; so that, by the expiration of a week, his career was brought to a close.

The termination of Bhaoji's career has been differently related. Nawab Shuja-ad-daulah, having mounted after the victory, took Shisha Dhar Pandit, Ganesh Pandit, and other associates of Bhaoji along with him and began wandering over the field of battle, searching for the corpses of the Maratha chiefs, and more especially for Bhaoji's dead body. They accordingly recognized the persons of Jaswant Rao Balwar, Pilaji, and Sabaji Nath, who had received forty sword-cuts, lying on the scene of action; and, in like manner, those of other famous characters also came in view. Bhao's corpse had not been found, when from beneath a dead body three valuable gems unexpectedly shone forth. The Nawab presented those pearls to the Pandits mentioned above, and directed them to try to recognize that lifeless form. They succeeded in doing so through the scar of a gunshot wound in the foot, and another on the side behind the back, which Bhao had received in former days. With their eyes bathed in tears they exclaimed: "This is Bhao, the ruler of the Deccan." Some entertain an opinion that Bhao, after Biswas Rao's death, performed prodigies of valour, and then disappeared from sight, and no one ever saw him afterwards. Two individuals consequently, both natives of the Deccan, publicly assumed the name of Bhao, and dragged a number of people into their deceitful snare. As a falsehood cannot bear the light, one was eventually put to death somewhere in the Deccan by order of the chiefs in that quarter, and the other, having excited an insurrection at Benares, was confined for some time in the fort of Chunar. After his release, despairing of the success of his project, he died in the suburbs of Gorakhpur in the year 1193 A. H. (1779 A. D.).

Nawab Shuja-ad-daulah Bahadur, having obtained permission of the Shah to burn the bodies of the Bhao and other chiefs, deputed Raja Himmat Bahadur and Rao Kashi Nath, his principal attendants, to perform the task of cremation. Out of all those hapless and unfortunate beings who survived the battle, a number maintained a precarious existence against the violent assaults of death for some days, but notwithstanding that they used the most strenuous exertions to effect their escape in divers directions from Panipat, not a single one was saved from being slain and plundered by the landlords of that quarter. Out of the whole of the celebrated chiefs too, with the exception of Malhar Rao Holkar, Appaji Gaikowar and Bithal Sudeo, not another was ever able to reach the Deccan.

Bhao's wife, in company with Shamsher Bahadur, half-brother to Balaji Rao, and a party of confidential attendants, traversed a long distance with the utmost celerity, and betook herself to the fortress of Dig. There that broken-hearted lady remained for two or three days mourning the loss of her husband, and having then made up her mind to prepare for an expedition to the Deccan, Raja Suraj Mal Jat gave her one morning a suitable escort to attend her, and bade her adieu. She accordingly reached the Deccan; but Shamsher Bahadur, who was severely wounded, died after arriving at Dig.

Shortly before the occurrence of these disasters, Balaji Rao had marched from Poona. He had proceeded only as far as Bhilsa, when, having been informed of the event, he grew wearied of existence, and shed tears of blood lamenting the loss of a son and a brother. He then moved from where he was to Sironj, and about that very time a messenger reached him from the Abdali Shah, with a robe of mourning. The Rao, feigning obedience to his commands, humbly dressed his person in the Shah's robe, and turning away from Sironj, re-entered Poona. From excess of grief and woe, however, he remained for two months afflicted with a harrowing disease; and as he perceived the image of death reflected from the mirror of his condition, he sent for his brother, Raghunath Rao, to whom he gave in charge his best-beloved son, the younger brother of the slain Biswas Rao, who bore the name of Madhu Rao, and had just entered his twelfth year, exclaiming: "Fulfil all the duties of good-will towards this fatherless child, treating him as if he were your own son, and do not permit any harm to come upon him." Having said this, he departed from the world on the 9th of Zi-al-kada, 1174 A. H. (June 14, 1761 A. D.), and the period of his reign was twenty-one years.

After the demise of his father, Madhu Rao was installed in the throne of sovereignty at Poona, and

THE GOPAL BHAWAN IN THE PALACE OF DIG.

Raghunath Rao conducted the administration of affairs as prime minister, after the manner of the late Bhao.

One of the remarkable incidents that occurred in Madhu Rao's reign was the appearance of a counterfeit Bhao, who, in the year 1175 A. H. (1762-3 A. D.), having induced a number of refractory characters to flock to his standard, and having collected together a small amount of baggage and effects, with camp equipage and cattle, excited an insurrection near the fort of Karaza, which is situated at a distance of twelve leagues from Jhansi towards the west. He gave intimation to the governor of the fort, who held his appointment of the Poona chiefs, as to his name and pretensions, and summoned him by threats and promises into his presence. The latter, who, up to that time, had been in doubt whether Bhao was dead or alive, being apprehensive lest this individual should in reality prove to be Bhao, proceeded to wait upon him, and presented some cash and valuables by way of offering. After that, the Bhao in question sent letters into other sub-districts, and having summoned the revenue officers from all quarters, commenced seizing and appropriating all the cash, property, and goods. Whatever horses, elephants, or camels he found with any one, he immediately sent for and kept in his own possession.

This pretender to the name of Bhao always kept his face half-covered under a veil, both in public and private, on the plea that the wound on his visage was still unhealed, and people were completely deceived by the stratagem; no one could have the impudence to scrutinize his features. In short, for six months he persevered in his imposture, until the news reached Poona, when some spies went over to him to examine strictly into the case, and discovered that he was not Bhao.

About the same period, Malhar Rao Holkar was

THE HILL OF PARVATI FROM THE LAKE, NEAR POONA.

moving from the Deccan towards Hindustan, and his road happened to lie through the spot where the pretender in question had pitched his tents. The spies already mentioned disclosed the particulars of the case to Malhar Rao, who thought to himself that until Parvati Bai, the late Bhao's wife, had seen this individual with her own eyes, and all her doubts had been removed, it would not do to inflict capital punishment on the impostor, for fear the lady should think in her heart that he had killed her husband out of spite and malice. For this reason, Malhar Rao merely took the impostor prisoner, and having appointed thirty or forty horsemen to take care of him, forwarded him from thence to Poona. The few weak-minded beings who had gathered round him were allowed to depart to their several homes, and Holkar proceeded to his destination. When the pretender was brought to Poona, Madhu Rao likewise, out of regard for the feelings of the late Bhao's wife, deemed it proper to defer his execution, and kept him confined in one of the forts within his own dominions. Strange to say, the silly people in that fort did not discover the falseness of the impostor's claims, and leagued themselves with him, so that a fresh riot was very nearly set on foot. Madhu Rao, however, having been apprised of the circumstances, sent him from that fort to another stronghold; and in the same way he was constantly transferred from various forts in succession, till he was finally confined in a stronghold that lies contiguous to the sea on the island of Kolaba, which is a dependency of the Konkan territory.

The following is another of the events of Madhu Rao's reign: Bithal, Minister of Finance to Nawab Nizam Ali Khan Bahadur, advised his master that as the Marathas were then devoid of influence, and the supreme authority was vested in an inexperienced child, it would be advisable to ravage Poona. Januji Bhonsla, Raja of Nagpur, Gopal Rao, a servant of the Peshwa, and some more chiefs of the Maratha nation, approved of this suggestion, and led their forces in a compact mass towards Poona. When they drew near its frontier, Raghunath Rao, who was Madhu Rao's chief agent and prime minister, got terrified at the enemy's numbers and, finding himself unable to cope with them, retired with his master from Poona. Nawab Nizam Ali Khan Bahadur then entered the city, and spared no efforts to complete its destruction.

After some time, Raghunath Rao recovered himself, and having entered into friendly communication with Januji Bhonsla and the other chiefs of his own tribe by opening an epistolary correspondence with them, he alienated the minds of these men from the Nawab. In short, the chiefs separated from the Nawab on pretence of the rainy season, and returned to their own territories. In the interim, Raghunath Rao and Madhu Rao set out to engage Nawab Nizam Ali Khan Bahadur, who, deeming it expedient to proceed to his original quarters, beat a retreat from the position he was occupying. When the bank of the river Godavari became the site of his encampment, an order was issued for the troops to cross over. Half the army was still on this side, and half on that, when Raghunath, considering it a favourable opportunity, commenced a furious onslaught. The six remaining chiefs of the Nawab's army were slain, and about seven thousand Afghans and others acquired eternal renown by gallantly sacrificing their lives. After this sanguinary conflict, the Nawab hastily crossed the river and extricated himself from his perilous position. As soon as the flame of strife had been extinguished, a peace was established through the intervention of Malhar Rao Holkar, who had escaped with his life in safety from the battle with Abdali Shah. Both parties, concurring in the advantages of an amicable understanding, returned to their respective quarters.

When Raghunath Rao began to usurp greater authority over the administration of affairs, Gopika Bai, Madhu Rao's mother, growing envious of his influence, inspired her son with evil suspicions against him, and planned several stratagems, so that their mutual friendship resulted in hatred and animosity, till at length Raghunath Rao became convinced that he would some day be imprisoned. Consequently, he mounted his horse one night, and fled precipitately from Poona with only a few adherents. Stopping at Nasik, which lies at a distance of eight stages from Poona, he fixed upon that town as his place of refuge and abode, and employed himself in collecting troops, insomuch that Naradji Sankar, the revenue collector of Jhansi, Jaswant Rao Lud, Sakha Ram Bapu, and Nilkanth Mahadeo volunteered to join him, and eagerly engaged in active hostilities against Madhu Rao. As soon as Raghunath Rao arrived in this condition close to Poona, Madhu Rao was also obliged to sally forth from it in company with Trimbak Rao, Bapuji Manik, Gopal Rao, and Bhimji Lamdi. When the line of battle began to be formed, Raghunath Rao assumed the initiative in attacking his adversaries, and succeeded in routing Madhu Rao's force by a series of overwhelming assaults; and even captured the Rao himself, together with Nar Singh Rao. After gaining this agreeable victory, as he perceived Madhu Rao to be in safety and his malicious antagonists overthrown, he could not contain himself for joy. As soon as he returned from the battle-field to his encampment, he seated Madhu Rao on a throne, and remained himself standing in front of him, after the manner of slaves. By fawning and coaxing, he then removed every trace of annoyance from Madhu Rao's mind, and requested him to return to Poona. After dismissing him to that city, he himself went with his retinue and soldiery to Nasik.

NASIK.

After the lapse of some years of Madhu Rao's reign, a vast disturbance arose in the Deccan. Haidar Naik, having assembled some bold and ferocious troops with intent to subdue the territory of the Marathas, set out in the direction of Poona. Madhu Rao came out from Poona, and summoned Raghunath Rao to his assistance from Nasik, whereupon the latter joined him with a body of twenty thousand of his cavalry. In short, they marched with their combined forces against the enemy; and on several occasions encounters took place, in which the lives of vast multitudes were destroyed. Although Haidar Naik's army proved itself superior in the field, yet peace was ultimately concluded on the cession and surrender of some few tracts in the royal dominions; after which Haidar Naik refrained from hostilities and returned to his own territory, while Madhu Rao retired to Poona, and Raghunath Rao betook himself to Nasik.

When a short time had elapsed after this, the idea of organizing the affairs of Hindustan entered into Raghunath Rao's mind. For the sake of preserving outward propriety, therefore, he first gave intimation to Madhu Rao of his intention, and asked his sanction. The Rao in question, who did not feel himself secure from Raghunath Rao, and considered any increase to his power a source of greater weakness to himself, addressed him a reply couched in these terms: "It were better for you to remain where you are, in the enjoyment of repose." Raghunath Rao would not listen to these words, but marched out of Nasik in company with Mahaji Sindhia, taking three powerful armies with him.

As soon as he reached Gwalior, he commenced hostilities against Rana Chattar Singh, who possessed all the country round Gohad, and laid siege to the town itself. Gohad is the name of a city, founded by the Rana aforesaid. It is fortified with earthen towers and battlements, and is situated eighteen leagues from Gwalior. Madhu Rao, during the continuance of the siege, kept constantly sending messages to Rana Chattar Singh, telling him to persist in his opposition to Raghunath with a stout heart, as the army of the Deccan should not be despatched to his kingdom to reinforce the latter. In a word, for the period of a year they used the most arduous endeavours to capture Gohad, but failed in attaining their object. During this campaign, the sum of 3,200,000 rupees, taken from the pay of the troops and the purses of the wealthy bankers, was incurred by Raghunath Rao as a debt to be duly repaid. He then returned to the Deccan distressed and overwhelmed with shame, and entered the city of Nasik, whither Madhu Rao also repaired about the same time, to see and inquire after his fortunes. In the course of the interview, he expressed the deepest regret for the toils and disappointment that the Rao had endured, and ultimately returned in haste to Poona, after thus sprinkling salt on the galling wound. Shortly after this, Kankuma Tantia and his other friends persuaded Raghunath Rao to adopt a Brahman's son. Accordingly the Rao attended to the advice of his foolish counsellors, and selected an individual for adoption. He constituted Amrat Rao his heir.

Madhu Rao no sooner became cognizant of this fact than he felt certain that Raghunath Rao was meditating mischief and rebellion, and seeking to usurp a share in the sovereignty of the realm. He consequently set out for Nasik with a force of twenty-five thousand horsemen, while, on the other hand, Raghunath Rao also organized his troops, and got ready for warfare. Just about that period, however, Kankuma Tantia and Takuji Holkar, who were two of the most powerful and influential men in Raghunath's army, declared to him that it was necessary for them to respect their former obligations to Madhu Rao, and therefore improper to draw the sword upon him. After a long altercation, they left the Rao where he was, and departed from Nasik. Raghunath, from the paucity of his troops, not deeming it advantageous to fight, preferred enduring disgrace, and fled with two thousand adherents to the fortress of Dhudhat in the Chandor range.

Madhu Rao then entered Nasik, and commenced sequestrating his property and imprisoning his partisans; after which he pitched his camp at the foot of the fort already mentioned, and placed Raghunath in a most precarious position. For two or three days the incessant discharge of artillery and musketry caused the flames of war to blaze high, but pacific negotiations were subsequently opened, and a firm treaty of friendship entered into, whereupon the Rao came down from the fort, and had an interview with Madhu Rao. The latter then placed his head upon the other's feet, and asked pardon for his offences. Next day, having mounted Raghunath Rao on his own private elephant, he himself occupied the seat usually assigned to the attendants, and continued for several days travelling in this fashion the distance to Poona. As soon as they entered Poona, Madhu Rao, imitating the behaviour of an inferior to a superior, exceeded all bounds in his kind and consoling attentions towards Raghunath Rao. After that he selected a small quantity of goods and a moderate equipment of horses and elephants, out of his own establishment, and having deposited them all together in one of the most lofty and spacious apartments, solicited Raghunath Rao in a respectful manner to take up his abode there. The latter then became aware of his being a prisoner with the semblance of freedom, and reluctantly complied with Madhu Rao's requisition.

As soon as Madhu Rao had delivered his mind from all apprehension regarding Raghunath Rao, he led his army in the direction of Nagpur, in order to avenge himself on Januji Bhonsla, the raja of that place, who had been an ally and auxiliary of Raghunath Rao in one of his engagements. The raja in question, not finding himself capable of resisting him, fled from his original residence, so that for a period of three months Madhu Rao was actively engaged in pursuing his adversary, and that unfortunate outcast from his native land was constantly fleeing before him. Ultimately, having presented an offering of a million and a half of rupees, he drew back his foot from the path of flight, and set out in safety and security for his own home.

After chastising the Raja of Nagpur, Madhu Rao entered Poona with immense pomp and splendour, and amused himself with gay and festive entertainments. But he was attacked with a fatal disease, and his life was in danger. On one occasion he laid his head on

Raghunath Rao's feet, and asked forgiveness for the faults of bygone days. Raghunath Rao grieved deeply on account of his youth. He applied himself zealously to the cure of the invalid, and whenever he found a trace, in any quarter or direction, of austere Brahmans and skilful Pandits, he sent for them to administer medicines for his recovery. At length, when the sick man began to despair of living, he imitated the example of his deceased father, and placed his younger brother, whose name was Narain Rao, under the charge of Raghunath Rao, and having performed the duty of recommending him to his care, yielded up his soul in the year 1186 A. H. (1772 A. D.). The duration of his reign was twelve years.

Narain Rao, after being seated on the throne of sovereignty, owing to his tender age committed various acts that produced an ill-feeling among his adherents, both great and small, at Poona; more especially in Raghunath Rao, on whom he inflicted unbecoming indignities. Although Madhu Rao had not behaved towards his uncle with the respect due to such a relative, yet, except that he would not grant him permission to leave Poona, he had treated him with no other incivility; but used always, till the day of his death, to show him the attention due from an inferior to a superior; and supplied him with wealth and property far exceeding the limits of his wants. In short, Raghunath Rao, having begun to form plans for taking Narain Rao prisoner, first disclosed his secret to Sakha Ram Bapu, who was Madhu Rao's prime minister, and having seduced that artless courtier from his allegiance, made him an accomplice in his treacherous designs. Secondly, having induced Kharak Singh and Shamsher Singh, the chiefs of the body of Gardis, or troops with European training, to join his conspiracy, he raised the standard of insurrection. Accordingly, these two faithless wretches one day, under the pretence of demanding pay for the troops, made an assault on the door of Narain Rao's apartment, and reduced him to great distress. That helpless being, who had not the slightest cognizance of the deceitful stratagems of the conspirators, sent a few simple-minded adherents to oppose the insurgents, and then stealthily repaired to Raghunath Rao's house. Kharak Singh and Shamsher Singh, being apprised of the circumstances, hurried after him, and, unsheathing their swords, rushed into Raghunath Rao's domicile. Raghunath Rao first fell wounded in the affray, and subsequently Narain Rao was slain. This event took place in the year 1187 A. H. (1773 A. D.), so that the period of Narain Rao's reign was one year.

AN INDIAN SCIMITAR.

Kharak Singh and Shamsher Singh, through whose brains the fumes of arrogance had spread in consequence of their control over the whole train of European artillery, with wilful and headstrong insolence seated Raghunath Rao on the throne of sovereignty, without the concurrence of the other chiefs; and the

Rao continued to live for two months at Poona after the manner of rightful rulers. When Narain Rao had been put to death, however, a certain degree of shame and remorse came over the Poona chiefs, and the dread of their own overthrow entered their minds. Sakha Ram Bapu consequently, in unison with Trimbak Rao, commonly called Matamadhari Balhah, and others, deemed it advisable to persuade Raghunath Rao that he should go forth from Poona, and employ himself in settling the kingdom. The Rao accordingly acted upon their suggestion, and marched out of Poona, attended by the Maratha chiefs. As soon as he had got to the distance of two or three stages from the city, the wily chiefs, by alleging some excuse, obtained leave from Raghunath Rao to return, and repaired from the camp to the city. They then summoned to them in private all the commanders of the army, both great and small, and came to the unanimous decision that it was incompatible with justice to acquiesce in Raghunath Rao's being invested with the supreme authority, and that it would be better, as Narain Rao's wife was six months advanced in pregnancy, providing she gave birth to a male child, to invest that infant with the sovereignty, and conduct the affairs of government agreeably to the details of prudence. As soon as they had unanimously settled the question after this fashion, a few of the chiefs took up a position in the outskirts of the city of Poona, by way of protection, and formed a sturdy barrier against the Magog of turbulence. Raghunath Rao, having become aware of the designs of the conspirators, remained with a slender party in his encampment. Having brooded over his troubles, he saw no remedy left but that of forsaking the country, and was consequently forced to retire towards the Carnatic. His object was to collect a sufficient force round him, with which he might return to Poona and resume hostilities. However, owing to the vulgar report that attributed Narain Rao's murder to him, every blade of grass that sprung from the ground was ready to plunge a dagger into his blood. For this reason, he found it impossible either to stay or reside in the Carnatic, so he hastened away to Surat.

The direst confusion had found its way into the kingdom, in consequence of the report of Narain Rao's death. At that critical juncture the pretender Bhao, who was confined in a stronghold in the Konkan territory, lying adjacent to the salt ocean, seized the opportunity of escaping by fraud and stratagem out of his prison, and having induced a party of men to place themselves under his orders, took possession of some of the forts and districts of that country. He was just on the point of waging open war, when Mahaji Sindhia Bahadur set out from Poona to the Konkan territory for the purpose of coercing him. On reaching his destination, he engaged in hostilities with Bhao, whereupon the latter's associates took to flight, and departed each by his own road. As Bhao was thus left alone, he went on board a ship in utter consternation with a view to save his life from that vortex of perdition; but death granted him no respite, and he fell alive into the hands of the heroes who accompanied Mahaji Sindhia Bahadur. The latter brought him along with him to Poona, and removed the dust of uncertainty from the mirror of every mind. Ultimately he caused the ill-fated wretch to be bound to a camel's foot, and paraded round the whole town; after which he put him to death.

The Peshwa Sahib, the rightful heir of Narain Rao, at the time of his father's murder was dwelling in his mother's womb. When she had completed the time of her pregnancy, a child, in the year 1188 A. H. (1774 A. D.), shed a grace over the bosom of its nurse, and bestowed comfort on the illustrious chiefs. He was invested with the appellation of Sawai Madhu Rao.

Raghunath Rao, having reached Surat, turned towards the leaders of the English army, who dwelt on the borders of the sea, and offered to take upon himself the responsibility of showing the way over the various routes into the Deccan, and to subjugate that kingdom so teeming with difficulties. As the commanders of the English army were possessed of adequate means for making an invasion, and had their heads inflamed with the intoxication of boldness and intrepidity, they took Raghunath Rao along with them, and moving away from Surat with their valiant troops experienced in war, and their lion-hearted forces active as tigers, they set out to conquer and annex the Deccan territories.

Having traversed the intervening stages at a resolute pace, they arrived at Nurghat, which is situated at a distance of twenty leagues from Poona. The Maratha chieftains also sallied forth from Poona with a vast body of retainers, and opposed their advance with the utmost perseverance at Nurghat; whereupon a tremendous cóntest and a frightful slaughter ensued, until the combatants on both sides had neither the power nor the inclination left to assail each other any more. At length, by the intervention of the obscurity of night, the tumult of war subsided, and the world-consuming fire of guns and matchlocks, whose flames arose to the highest heavens, hid its face in the ashes of night, so that the soldiery was obliged to retire, each to its respective quarters. During that night, the prudent belligerents made up their minds to a peace; and in the morning, the chiefs of the rival forces obtained an interview and enjoyed a conference. The English leaders, after negotiating a truce and consolidating the basis of friendship, delivered up Raghunath Rao, who had been the instigator of this conflict and the originator of this hostile movement, to the Maratha chiefs, on condition of their granting him certain lands and rents as an annuity, and treating him with kindness and consideration. They then turned away from that quarter with all their troops and followers, and repaired to their usual place of abode.

The Maratha chiefs had formed the fixed determination in their minds of taking vengeance on the ill-fated Raghunath Rao; but Mahaji Sindhia Bahadur, prompted by his manly and generous feelings, diverted them from their headlong and cruel purposes, so that the matter was managed mercifully and kindly, and the

Rao in question, having been presented with an annuity, received permission to remain at large. The unfortunate wretch, however, departed from the pleasant vale of existence to the desert of nonentity, without reaching his destination, for the career of the wicked never ends well.

When the fourth year from the birth of Sawai Madhu Rao, surnamed the Peshwa Sahib, had elapsed, and security and repose had settled on the minds of high and low throughout the territory of the Deccan, Mahaji Sindhia Bahadur, who was distinguished among all the Poona chiefs for his gallantry and daring, sagacity and intelligence, having satisfied his mind as to the settlement of that kingdom, set out to conquer Gohad. After a siege attended with hard fighting, he succeeded in taking prisoner Rana Chattar Singh, who was in the citadel, and took possession of the surrounding districts, along with the fortress of Gwalior, which is a mountain stronghold.

About the same time, a mutual feeling of envy and hatred had become firmly implanted in the minds of Mirza Muhammad Shafi Khan and Muhammad Beg Khan Hamadani, who had been the chief officers of State to the late "Amir of amirs" Mirza Najaf Khan Bahadur, and after his death had been partners in the government of the province of Agra, since each craved after an increase of power and dignity, which is ever a hindrance to the existence of friendship and good feeling among equals and contemporaries. At last, Muhammad Beg Khan Hamadani seized the opportunity, during an interview, of putting Muhammad Shafi Khan to death; and on this account, Afrasiyab Khan, who was one of Mirza Najaf Khan Bahadur's *protégés*, becoming alarmed, demanded succour of Mahaji Sindhia Bahadur. The latter had firmly resolved in his mind to repair to the sublime threshold, but had not yet fulfilled the duty of paying his respects, when, under the influence of Sindhia Bahadur's destiny, Afrasiyab Khan was killed by the hand of an assassin.

Sindhia Bahadur's army having overshadowed the metropolis by its arrival, he brought Muhammad Beg Khan Hamadani, after a siege, completely under his subjection, and in the year 1199 A. H. (1784 A. D.) traversed the streets of the metropolis. When he obtained the good fortune of saluting the threshold of his Majesty, the shadow of God, the Emperor Shah Alam, he was loaded with princely favours and distinguished by royal marks of regard, so that he became the chief of the supporters of government and his Majesty's most staunch and influential adherent.

As at the present auspicious period Madhu Rao, the Peshwa Sahib, pursues, in contradistinction to his uncle, the path of obedience to the monarch of Islam, and Mahaji Sindhia Bahadur is one of those who are constantly attached to the ever-triumphant train, it happens that the plant of this nation's prosperity has struck root firmly into the earth of good fortune, and their affairs flourish agreeably to their wishes.

APPENDIX III

CHRONOLOGICAL SUMMARY

A.D.

1556 Battle of Panipat: Akbar king of Delhi.

1560–2 Jaunpur, Malwa, Burhanpur annexed.

1567 Akbar storms Chitor.

1569 Founding of Fathpur-Sikri.

1572–3 Gujarat annexed.

1574 The Hall of Worship built at Fathpur-Sikri.

1575 Conquest of Bengal.

1582 Todar Mal makes a new assessment of lands.

1587 Kashmir, 1592 Sind, 1594 Kandahar annexed.

1599 Conquest of Ahmadnagar in the Deccan.

1600 Conquest of Asir in Khandesh.

1600 Incorporation of the first East India Company.

1605 Death of Akbar.

1609–11 Hawkins at the court of Jahangir: English factory at Surat.

1615–18 Sir Thomas Roe's embassy to Jahangir.

1616 Shah Jahan's campaign in the Deccan.

1622 Kandahar taken by Persia, recovered 1637, lost again 1648.

1623 Pietro della Valle in India.

1624 Rebellion of Shah Jahan against Jahangir and Nur Jahan.

1627 Death of Jahangir.

1631 Suppression of the Portuguese at Hugli.

1635 Shah Jahan reduces Bijapur to tributary dependence.

1638 Mandelslo at Agra.

1640 Manrique in India.

1646 Death of Nur Jahan.

1648 Completion of the Taj Mahal at Agra.

A. D.	
1648	New Delhi, Shahjahanabad, built.
1648	Sivaji raids the Konkan.
1649–52	Aurangzib fails to recover Kandahar from the Persians.
1655	Aurangzib viceroy in the Deccan.
1656	Golkonda attacked; Bidar and Kulbarga annexed.
1658	War of succession: battle of Samugarh.
1659	Accession of Aurangzib: death of Shah Jahan, 1666.
1659–66	Bernier at the court of Aurangzib.
1665	Tavernier in India.
1666	Suppression of Portuguese pirates in Arakan.
1671	Sivaji sacks Surat: Marathas supreme in the Deccan.
1672	Satnami rebellion in Mewat.
1676	Reimposition of the jizya, or poll-tax.
1680	War with the Rajputs.
1681	Aurangzib takes command against the Marathas.
1686	Fall of Bijapur, and 1687 of Golkonda.
1695	Gemelli Careri at Aurangzib's camp in the Deccan.
1707	Death of Aurangzib.
1708	Revolt of the Sikhs.
1738	The Marathas advance to Delhi.
1739	Nadir Shah sacks Delhi.
1748	Afghan invasion under Ahmad Shah routed at Sirhind.
1756	Ahmad Shah sacks Delhi.
1757	Battle of Plassey: Clive defeats the Nawab.
1761	Battle of Panipat: defeat of the Marathas.
1764	Battle of Baxar: the Great Moghul becomes a pensioner of the East India Company.

APPENDIX IV

MOGHUL EMPERORS[1]

932	Babar	1526
937	Humayun	1530
946	Humayun deposed by Sher Shah	1539
962	Humayun restored	1555
963	Akbar	1556
1014	Jahangir	1605
1037	Shah Jahan	1628
1069	Aurangzib 'Alamgir	1659
1119	Bahadur	1707
1124	Jahandar	1712
1124	Farrukhsiyar	1713
1131	Mohammad	1719
1161	*Invasion of Ahmad Shah Durrani*	1748
1161	Ahmad	1748
1167	'Alamgir II	1754
1173	Shah 'Alam	1759
1221	Mohammad Akbar II	1806
1253	Bahadur	1837
1275	*Queen Victoria*	1857

[1] For several pretenders and ephemeral or local sovereigns of this line see Lane-Poole, *The Mohammedan Dynasties*, 328.

TREE OF THE MOGHUL EMPERORS

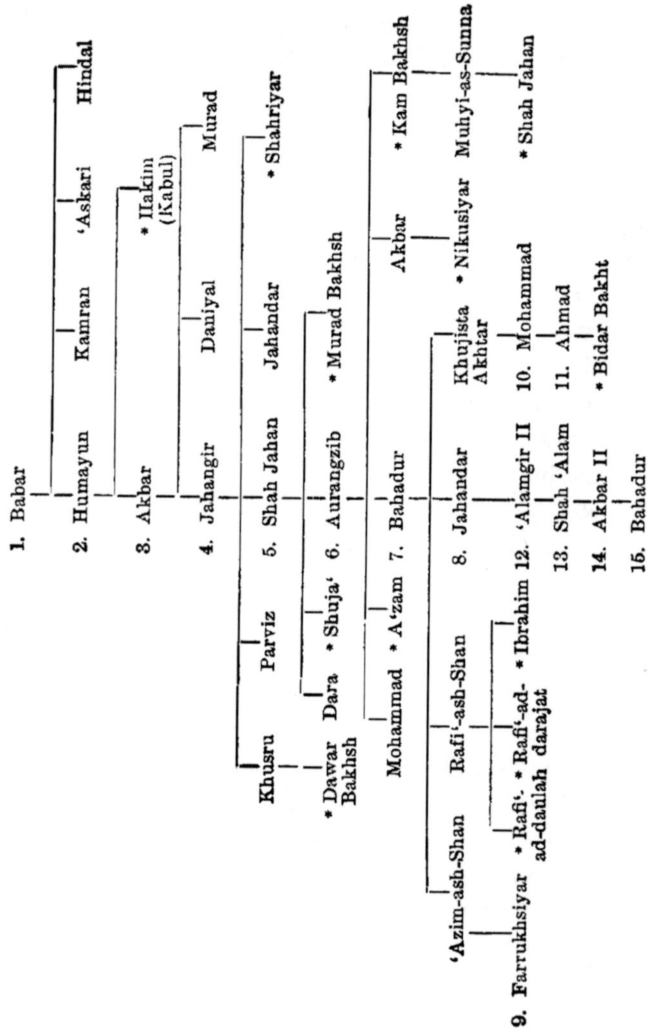

* The princes marked with an asterisk were proclaimed emperors either as temporary stop-gaps or rivals to the reigning emperor, but cannot be said to have reigned.

INDEX

B

C

E

F

G

H

Published by

Facsimile Publisher
Ashok Vihar, Delhi-110052 (India)
Website: www.facsimilepublisher.com

Distributed by

Gyan Books Pvt. Ltd.
5, Ansari Road, Daryaganj, New Delhi-110002 (India)
E-mail: books@gyanbooks.com, Website: www.gyanbooks.com

8 888000 714552